CRUISING NORWAY
2017-18

CONTENTS

Introduction	3
Cruising Options for Norway	6
Geography of Norway	11
A Norwegian History	21
Oslo - The National Metropolis and Capital	27
Stavanger	45
Haugesund	57
Bergen - Norway's Second City	66
Sognefjord - Visiting Fläm and Gudvangen	82
Nordfjorden - Visiting Olden	94
Ålesund	103
Storfjorden - Visiting Hellesylt and Geiranger	118
Kristiansund	129
Trondheimsfjorden - VisitingTrondheim	143
The Lofoten Islands - Visiting Svolvær	155
Harstad	164
Tromsø	170

Alta	**182**
Hammerfest	**189**
Honningsvag and Nordkapp	**197**
Cruising to Murmansk and Arkhangelsk, Russia	**203**
About the Author	**224**

The majority of maps used in this book are from Open Street Map contributors and are so noted for each map. For further information contact: www.OpenStreetMap.org/copyright

INTRODUCTION

A map of Norway and Svalbard

After cruising Norway for the past ten years, and having visited all of the major ports of call along its long and convoluted coastline, I finally feel it is time to present this book on Cruising Norway. Of all the places in the world where the cruise industry has developed itineraries, none can compare with the raw natural landscapes of intense beauty combined with the romantic Viking history that are found in Norway, one of the most sought after travel destinations for those who love to travel by ship.

This book provides you with an overview of Norway of its physical characteristics and challenging geography and a moderately detailed history to enable you to best appreciate the country without having to delve into complex academic treatises on either subject. Often my readers ask me to add more minute geographic or historic detail, but for me to do so, I am simply repeating what is already in the literature. The aim of this book is to enable you to gain a sufficient understanding of the physical and cultural landscapes of Norway to then focus upon the enjoyment of the ports of call your cruise includes, not to be able to pass a college exam on the subject.

I have included all of the primary ports of call visited by the major cruise lines, but have left out those minor ports that can only be visited utilizing the local ferry boats or combined mail/passenger services that ply the hundreds of small fjords and bays, connecting nearly every significant village with the rest of the country. This book gives the reader the essentials on the important ports that are likely to be a part of the itineraries of the well-known cruise lines.

I trust you will find this book both informative and sufficiently enticing to whet your appetite for a cruise along the coast and through the fjords of Norway.

Dr. Lew Deitch,
April 2017

Morning mist lingers over Geirangerfjorden

CRUISING OPTIONS FOR NORWAY

Most of the major cruise lines offer summertime Norwegian Fjord itineraries. These cruise lines vary in price and of course in the levels of quality service and cuisine being offered. The itineraries vary from short one-week cruises to two weeks or longer. I strongly recommend cruise itineraries that are devoted only to the Norwegian ports and that begin and terminate either in Copenhagen or Oslo. In this way you are not spending days at sea between such starting or ending ports as Southampton, Edinburgh or Amsterdam. Why spend time at sea that could be better spent in Norway. You must choose your cruise line and the itinerary carefully to maximize how much of the country you will see, recognizing that Norway is so vast that you cannot get more than an introduction to its land and people on a single cruise. After ten years of cruising Norway, there are still a handful of ports capable of hosting a cruise ship that I have not visited.

Your choice of cruise line must be guided by the following factors to maximize your enjoyment:
* The amount of time you wish to spend on the cruise. The longer the time frame, the more ports of call and fjords you can visit. With the majority of cruises starting in Oslo, Copenhagen or Bergen, a minimum of two weeks is needed to explore well north into the Arctic region of Norway.
* The level of luxury and the number of on board amenities are important factors. The most luxurious ships are primarily found in the fleets of Silversea, Seaborne and Regent. These ships are relatively small and can offer more detailed itineraries that include ports seldom if ever visited by the larger cruise ships. The higher end cruise lines offer staterooms that are generally larger and better appointed than the mega ships belonging to the major mass market companies. There is also a higher ratio of crewmembers to passengers, thus giving more personalized and attentive service. Likewise the cuisine on the smaller up market lines is gourmet oriented, and often provides a taste of the countries being visited. But because these ships are smaller and carry fewer passengers their theaters and casinos are likewise not overly large and the entertainment is not as lavish. One must choose between having a more sedate and elegant atmosphere or "glitz" and glamour of the larger vessels.
* The level of detail that you wish to experience is a guiding factor. For the most intensive look at the more remote locations in Norway, there are a few adventure cruise ships that will offer itineraries that visit the most inaccessible ports or fjords that are not visited by either large or luxury cruise ships. Also Norway's Hurtigruten line offers the most extensive itineraries on its local mail runs and adventure oriented cruise ships. They also offer cruises during

the winter months, a time when the majority of travelers are looking at tropical itineraries.

For those who are new to cruising or who have not traveled to Norway, here are some basic tips that will help to maximize your voyage:
* Always book an outside cabin if traveling on one of the larger ships that offer less expensive interior cabins, which have neither a window nor a veranda. Interior cabins can be quite claustrophobic because it is always necessary to use artificial illumination. At night these cabins are totally dark to where a nightlight is needed in the event you want to get out of bed for any reason. And without at least a window, you will miss so much of the local scenery in transit between ports of call. Much of the joy in cruising Norway is to just sit and soak in the passing scenery. Remember that daylight hours are extensive and much of the time you are close to the shore, traveling the inside passages or within the fjords.
* To economize, book an outside cabin with a window, as these are generally on the lower passenger decks where a veranda is not provided. One advantage in rough seas is that being lower down in the ship equals more stability when the ship begins to pitch or roll. There are often rough waters in the North Sea, especially on the transit between the northern tip of Denmark and the southern coast of Norway.
* Although forward lower deck cabins are offered at the lowest prices, be aware that the ship's maneuvering thrusters and anchors are forward. You will be exposed to a fair amount of noise when the ship is entering or leaving a harbor, rotating its position prior to docking and during docking maneuvers, and this can often interrupt your morning sleep, especially if you tend to be a light sleeper.
* If having the opportunity to enjoy fresh air at any time is important to you, then it is wise to book a cabin with a veranda. And while traveling in Norway there is often so much scenery to be enjoyed from your cabin while in transit between ports.
* Whenever possible book a cabin in mid ship, as when a ship begins to pitch the mid section acts like the fulcrum in that it experiences far less movement than either forward or aft cabins. The North Sea is noted for squalls that can cause the sea to become choppy. Once inside the fjords, the seas are generally exceptionally calm.
* If you should become queasy during periods of rough weather and pitching or rolling sea, it is best to go up on deck or out on your verandah and breath some fresh air. Also by staring off at the horizon the body surprisingly is less stressed by motion. But if you are unable to go out on deck because of the danger presented during really inclement weather, it is still possible to sit near a window and from time to time look out to sea, toward the horizon. Fear also

plays a role in the way you feel during rough seas. If you become frightened that the ship may capsize or sink, it will only heighten your feeling of uneasiness. Remember that ships can take a lot of punishment, and it is rare for a modern cruise liner to go down in rough weather. Starving one's self when feeling queasy will only make the condition worse. Dry crackers or toast along with hot tea is one way to calm an irritated stomach. And there are patches, pills or injections available from the ship's medical office to calm extreme discomfort.

* Be prepared for sudden changes in the weather. During summertime, the average temperatures in Norway are in the teens or very low 20's Celsius, which is between 50 and 75 degrees Fahrenheit. Occasional summer rainstorms can drop temperatures and it is easy to become chilled or soaked if not properly dressed or carrying an umbrella. Dressing in layers is the best way to accommodate the changes that can occur on a given day. And yes there are occasional hot, humid days when the sky is blue, the sun feels strong and temperatures can climb up to between 25 and 30 degrees Celsius, which is between 77 and 86 degrees Fahrenheit, but these are the exception rather than the rule.

* Do not over indulge in eating or drinking. It is best to pace yourself and try and eat normally, as you would at home. Overindulgence only leads to discomfort and added weight gain. And even though meals are included on board ship, one of the delights is in having a meal ashore. Norway is noted for its fresh fish and seafood. And Norwegian cuisine is elegantly prepared and one of the delights of the country.

* When in port, weight the option of going on organized tours against freelancing and visiting on your own. If you have any sense of adventure, a local map, public transit information and the names of basic venues make it possible to see as much, if not more, in a relaxed atmosphere in contract to being shepherded around as part of a tour group. Also by striking off on your own you have more opportunity to mingle with and meet local residents. And in Norway most people do speak English as their second language, with many also speaking German. But in some of the more remote locations or smaller villages the only option is to take organized tours offered by your cruise line, as local tour operators are few in number.

When starting a cruise, arrive at least 24 hours ahead of the departure and spend a minimum of one night in the port of embarkation. This enables you to recover from jet lag and to become acclimated to a new environment.

* When disembarking, it is also recommended that you spend at least one night in the final port of call before flying home. Two nights is preferable if your port of departure is either Copenhagen or Oslo.

When on shore in Norway it is safe to eat without fear of gastrointestinal upset. The country maintains a high degree of sanitation, and good restaurants abound. And drinking the local water is totally safe even though most restaurants offer bottled water.

* Violent crime in Norway is rare. The ports of call on the itineraries are exceptionally safe. However, pickpockets are found almost everywhere in the major cities such as Copenhagen, Oslo, Bergen and Trondheim where tourists will be seen in greater numbers. So wise precautions always apply regarding not keeping a wallet in a back pocket, not showing large sums of money and for women to keep a tight reign on their handbags.

* The use of credit cards is widespread at all major restaurants and shops. However, in Europe data chips are the norm. If your credit card has a data chip, insert it into the front of the credit card machine and follow the prompts. You will either enter a pin code or wait for the receipt to be issued and then sign it. Cards without a data chip will require a special pin code. Check with your credit card service before leaving.

* In Norway the national currency is the Norwegian Kroner. The use of the Euro, Pound or other foreign currency is rare, and only the occasional tourist oriented shop may be willing to accept other currencies. It is best to obtain Norwegian Kroner at an ATM or currency exchange at the start of your cruise. The easiest option is to order it in advance from your personal bank at home before departing.

Returning to the ship is normally expedited by having your cruise identification card handy to be swiped by the security officers. Packages and large handbags are often put through an x-ray machine similar to what is used at airports. And passengers pass through an arch to screen for any major metal objects.

Most ships offer hand sanitizers at the gangway and recommend that you sanitize your hands upon return. This is not mandatory, but it never hurts to be cautious. Norway is one of the cleanest countries in the world, but still a bit of extra precaution is a good policy.

The Norwegian Kroner comes in the following denominations of graduated sizes and there are coins for values below 50 Kroner

GEOGRAPHY OF NORWAY

The topography of Norway with its coastline of fjords and offshore islands. (Maps of Europe, Creative Commons Attribution Share Alike 3.0 license)

Norway is the westernmost nation of the Scandinavian Peninsula with its southern coast on the Kattegat and Skagerrak, a waterway that is actually an extension of the North Sea. However, historically Norway, Denmark and Sweden have been interwoven throughout time and even today there are close bonds between the three nations that consider themselves to be the heartland

of Scandinavia.

Geographically Norway is considered to be an elongated nation, essentially meaning that its shape has one axis that is far greater than the other. In this case, the north to south distance across Norway averages nearly 1,800 kilometers (1,100 miles) while its east to west extent in the south is less than 200 kilometers (120 miles). In the far north there are locations where the country is less than 100 kilometers (60 miles) in width. Given its highly indented coastline and nearly 50,000 offshore islands, the total Norwegian coastline is nearly 22,000 kilometers (13,620 miles) in length.

The total land area of Norway covers 323,802 square kilometers (125,000 square miles), which is approximately the size of the American state of New Mexico. But it is the elongated shape that makes the country appear to be so much larger than its total land area indicates. Norway extends over 13 degrees of latitude, extending north to just over 71 degrees North Latitude, making it the most northerly location in all of Europe. Approximately one third of the length of Norway extends north of the Arctic Circle, giving this region 24 hours of total daylight for nearly two months and then a reversal in winter with 24 hours of total darkness. In actuality, all of Norway experiences long summer days and long winter nights.

Norway's total population is only 5.207.689 (as estimated in 2015 by the CIA World Factbook). Over 1,000,000 live in the greater Oslo region.

THE NORWEGIAN LANDSCAPE: Norway is essentially a mountainous country, one of the most rugged countries in Europe with over 70 percent of the country consisting of mountain slopes. Only 2.7 percent of the country is considered to be arable, yet the Norwegians are able to develop pastures and orchards along with small garden plots on slopes that seem to be impossible to access. This is also a nation in which over 2/3 of the land is raw wilderness, so steep or so far north and cold that it has not been settled. And the combination of high altitude and high latitude, especially north of the Arctic Circle also means that much of the land is above the tree line, and sits bare and windswept.

The Scandinavian Mountains serve as the backbone or spine of the nation with spurs extending both east and west from the central ridges. The highest peak reaches an elevation of 2,469 meters (8,100 feet) above sea level. The median elevation of the land is just over 460 meters (1,500 feet). These are old mountains that share a common thread with the mountains of the British Isles and the Appalachians of North America. It is believed that they once were part of the ancient continent of Pangaea prior to its breaking apart to slowly form the continents we know today. These mountains were heavily glaciated during the Ice Age or Pleistocene, as much of the land was buried under more than a kilometer of ice. As the ice advanced and retreated four times over several million years, it sculpted and gouged deepened former river valleys along with grinding down and sharpening many of the highest peaks. The landscapes of Norway are among the most spectacular and beautiful of any nation. This is a country of superlatives. The Scandinavian Mountains extend the entire length of the nation and are broken by deep valleys that once carried glaciers down to the sea during the four great glacial advances. In the far north, there are still many small active glaciers to this day. As the glacial ice sculpted these deep valleys, they were turned from "V" shape river valleys into wide "U" shape gashes through the scour and pressure exerted by the moving ice. Very steep nearly vertical walls leading up to the higher peaks are the hallmarks of glacially created valleys. As the sea level rose with the last glacial retreat, many of the high mountaintops were left standing as islands while these deeply carved valleys flooded with seawater to form the magnificent Norwegian fjords. Thus present-day Norway has a coastline that is over 25,000 kilometers (15,600 miles) in length when one considers every mile of deeply indented channels called fjords and all of the islands. This same action occurred along the coastline of Alaska and British Columbia as well as in southern Chile and on South Island New Zealand. And today fjords are being carved by glacial action on Greenland and Canada's Baffin Island. But of all the glacially created fjords, none have the combined physical and cultural magnificence of those in Norway. This is not to say that the other fjords are not beautiful because of course they are. But there is a quality to the Norwegian fjords that is hard to match, even harder to put into words.

Most of southern and central Norway is covered in dense forest, the same coniferous forest that stretches into Russia, known as the taiga. Stands of spruce, pine and willow dominate the lower elevations, as at these northern latitudes the tree line is not very high above sea level. However, in the far north, above the Arctic Circle where the long winter climate is harsh, the landscape is one of tundra, essentially a polar desert. Norway's population clings to the shoreline and occupies the small valleys in between the higher peaks, but this leaves them with very little land that is good for farming. Yet the Norwegians are excellent farmer, working what they have to produce dairy products, fruits and vegetables.

Norway is rich in raw material resources. It is obvious that timber has been one resource, but the North Sea shoreline is exceptionally well endowed with reserves of oil and natural gas. There are also deposits of copper, lead, zinc and titanium that have added to Norway's overall mineral wealth. However, to mine these resources, the Norwegians have been forced exploit remote mountain areas, and for the extraction of oil and natural gas they have had to build some of the tallest off shore drilling platforms ever constructed. Norway is also well known for its shipbuilding and fishing industries, thus the technology was there to turn to building oil-drilling platforms. Many ocean liners and cargo ships have been built in Norway, and Norwegian corporations have invested heavily in the shipping industry.

Norway is a country dominated over by winter. Around the Atlantic coastal margins rain rather than snow predominates because of the moderating influence of the warmer waters of the Gulf Stream. But even at sea level, the winter have periods of time that experience occasional heavy snow showers. The climate is said to be maritime, influenced heavily by the sea. The mountains and the interior experience cold winter temperatures and heavy snowfall. And most of Norway experiences little to no daylight for approximately two months in the middle of winter. Summer days are long; full 24 hours north of the Arctic Circle. And temperatures are mild, but along the coast there is still frequent rainfall, occasional fog and many days where there is no sunshine. Many coastal communities average only about 30 percent of the days in a calendar year during which there will be sunshine.

With a wet climate and high rugged mountain slopes, Norway is blessed with fast flowing rivers and streams, most flowing with tremendous force of white water rapids. Where rivers plunge over the glacially carved walls of the fjords, thousands of waterfalls add to the overall drama of the landscape.

At these northern latitudes during the long winter nights, Norwegians are treated to an incredible light show, as the Aurora Borealis; also known as the Northern Lights, dance across the sky. Many visitors wait until the deepest part of winter and willingly brave the cold, rain and snow to have an opportunity to witness this phenomena so widely associated with Norway. But of course it is also visible in neighboring Sweden as well as in Finland, Russia, Alaska, Canada and Greenland.

Tourism plays a significant role in the Norwegian economy. During the summer, there are increasingly more and more cruise ships that offer tours along and through the fjords. Also the extensive Norwegian ferry system transports tens of thousands of European and American visitors along this spectacular coastline, some coming by automobile and combining road and ferry to explore even the most remote of those fjords that are serviced.

The small and rugged mountains along the coast near Bergen

Small shelves of gentle land for farming on the offshore Lofoten Islands

A thundering white water river flows past the village of Hellesylt

The lower reaches of the Geiranger River just above where it enters the Geiranger Fjord.

The spectacular beauty of Nærøyfjorden in central Norway

The upper reaches of the Valley of Fläm that was glacially carved

The high glacially sculpted mountains above Olden on Nordfjorden

The inside passage north of the city of Tromsø

The high and bleak tundra landscape of Magerøya Island on the Arctic shore

The Sámi people graze their reindeer on the Arctic islands and peninsula

A NORWEGIAN HISTORY

To best understand the culture and the landscape of any country visited, it is important to know something of its history. It is the course of history that molds the culture, creates the visual landscape with regard to both the physical and human elements seen. Architecture, transportation networks, farming patterns and the amount of natural forest or grassland are all impacted by the succession of events that took place in the past. And for this reason history plays a major role in what the visitor encounters. In the case of Norway, this is an old country with regard to a history that extends back to the 9th century, yet as a modern nation, it only dates to 1905.

To many future visitors, the name Norway is often synonymous with those northern warriors known as the Vikings. In essence it is their history that is the starting point for any written account of Norwegian timelines, yet there were earlier fishing and hunting tribes living along its shores dating back into prehistoric times. Despite the Hollywood image of the Vikings as warriors who terrorized and pillaged the shores of northern Europe, there were also merchants who engaged in legitimate trade, and colonists who set out from their cold, windswept lands to find more suitable homes.

Initially the Viking populace was scattered into tribal groups, each with its own chief of king. But in 872, much of the country was united under King Harald Hårfagre, this being the start of what would become a powerful force in Scandinavia. The Vikings adhered to their traditional "pagan" beliefs, but by the 11th century, Christian teaching had ultimately converted the majority, also helping to stem their raids on the nations along the North Sea.

The Kalmar Union, which was propagated by the Danes in 1350, ultimately united Norway and Sweden into one confederation, which was under the rule of a single king. But the Swedes rebelled in 1523 and left the Union because of their dissatisfaction with the power of the Danish crown. This break up was not without its share of bloodshed. Norway then became relegated to the status of a mere Danish province, something the Norwegians greatly resented. This displeasure festered until 1814, when Denmark, having lost a war with France, was forced to surrender Norway to Swedish rule. The Norwegians had drafted a constitution for their independence, but although forced into union with Sweden, many provisions of that draft were put into effect, as Sweden gave Norway a certain degree of internal home rule and its own separate crown, but the king was of Swedish nationality

As a means of fostering nationalism, the Norwegian people turned inward and concentrated their efforts upon fostering greater interest in their cultural identity through the arts, music and other manifestations of what it meant to be Norwegian. But ultimately this led to a political interest in the creation of an independent nation, which finally came to fruition on 7th July 1905 when the Norwegian Storting declared the country separated from Sweden and that the Swedish crown no longer would be recognized. The Swedish government was livid and there were even calls for armed forces to be sent into Norway. But in the end, both countries held separate referenda, and Norwegian independence was approved.

Since there was no Norwegian royal house, it was decided to invite young Prince Carl of Denmark, son of King Christian IX, to become the king of Norway. Taking the traditional Norwegian name of Haakon, the new royal house was established. And King Haakon VII reigned until 1957. To the present day, King Haarald V is the true head of the royal family, but also shows pride in his close familial relationship to the Danish Royal Family.

Life for the average Norwegian during the 19th and early 20th century was hard, as the country's economy was based upon limited farming, timber extraction and fishing. Essentially Norway was a backward country and large numbers of the poor emigrated primarily to Canada and the United States. It has been estimated that well over half a million Norwegians left for the New World, and states such as Minnesota, North and South Dakota and the Canadian provinces of Ontario and Manitoba show significant Norwegian communities. As in many European countries, manufacturing plants were developing in the major cities, and for those peasants who left the land for the city, life remained hard, often more difficult because urban residents were not able to at least supplement their incomes with homegrown foods.

Unlike many countries in Europe that industrialized, Norway did have one ready source of power, that being hydroelectric that provided clean and affordable energy for both industrial and domestic use. Apart from shipbuilding, manufacturing of paper products and a few fine quality metallic implements, Norway did not become one of Europe's industrial giants.

Although Norway was not drawn into the First World War, its economy did feel the same degree of contraction during the global depression of the 1930's. At the outbreak of World War II, Norway was invaded by Nazi forces from Germany because it offered two important resources. Its hydroelectric facilities, especially in the southern part of the country, were necessary for the production of heavy water, a vital component for the possible creation of nuclear weapons. And secondly was Norway's coastline that fronted on the major warm water trade route to the far north of European Russia. Nazi submarines and planes could harass allied shipping meant to aid the Russians in its fight on the Eastern Front once Germany invaded the Soviet Union.

The German invasion of Norway overwhelmed the small Norwegian military and the country fell under Nazi occupation, but a strong resistance movement developed and was instrumental in thwarting many of Germany's strategic operations. Sweden offered refuge to the Norwegian freedom fighters along with Allied pilots and paratroopers who aided in operations against Nazi installations.

Germany established a puppet government under the leadership of Vidkun Quisling, a man whose very name became associated with being a traitor to one's own country. But the vast majority of Norwegians silently opposed German occupation even though Nazi propaganda tried to equate being Norwegian with being a part of their so-called "master race." The Viking heritage of Norway figured prominently into Nazi myth.

Modern Norway presents a totally different picture than it did in pre war years. After two decades of reconstruction and repair of many damaged bridges, roads and harbor installations because of the war, Norway was soon back to a level of economic stability. The country took its place in the modern world as a member of the United Nations and later of the North Atlantic Treaty Organization.

The biggest single boost to Norway was the discovery of oil and natural gas in large underwater reserves off the coast, but within Norwegian territorial limits. As a result, the country with its small population began to see great sums of money coming into its treasury. Rather than utilizing the money for infrastructure or squandering it on monumental constructs, Norway invested the money in global programs for the benefit of its citizens in a national pension program. Today Norway's pension program is the envy of the world, and every one of its citizens has a secure future ahead. Infrastructure development, medical and educational services and other government programs are financed through high levels of taxation while the pension program is the beneficiary of the petroleum and gas profits. Even with the current low prices for fossil fuels, Norway is secure. However, jobs in the petroleum and gas industry have diminished, and this has caused unemployment that then strains the government's welfare programs.

Overall life in Norway is good. There is equal pay for men and women, excellent health and welfare benefits, and the country has a strong educational system available to all citizens. Yet Norwegians are not overly indulgent and the average family lives a comfortable lifestyle without being extravagant, as seen among other oil rich nations. Norwegians hold the natural environment to be very special, and they enjoy their country's beauty and recreational potential. It is true that there is no "Eden" on this earth, but Norway is one of those countries where life can be described as almost idyllic.

Akershus Castle in Oslo dates to 1290 AD

Hanseatic League buildings in Bergen date to the 14th century

The old village church in Geiranger

Interior of the old village church in Olden

OSLO - THE NATIONAL METROPOLIS AND CAPITAL

Oslo Fjord (© OpenStreetMap contributors)

Oslo Fjord and the city of Oslo. (© OpenStreetMap contributors)

A map of metropolitan Oslo. (© OpenStreetMap contributors)

A map of the city center of Oslo. (© OpenStreetMap contributors)

THE SETTING FOR OSLO: Cruise ships do not visit Oslo as often as the other major cities of Scandinavia or the Baltic Sea region. The itineraries of the major cruise lines seem to leave out Oslo more often than they do include it. The city's location is not as pivotal as Copenhagen or Stockholm in the planning of cruise itineraries. A visit to Oslo often involves one day or a half-day at sea at both the front and back end of the port call because of its location easily worked into a seven or 10-day cruise schedule.

Norway's capital is located approximately 130 kilometers (80 miles) up the long and narrow Oslofjord, which was created by glacial action during the Pleistocene or Ice Age. The journey up the fjord as well as back out after visiting the city is one of the highlights of visiting Oslo by ship. There are many small villages with their whitewashed wood houses that cling to the forested hillsides overlooking the fjord. It takes around three hours sailing time to reach the city or the Skagerrak on the return voyage. And if the weather is good, sitting out on deck and watching the passing countryside is richly rewarding, as it gives you a good glimpse into life in coastal life in the more populated portion of southern Norway.

Oslo occupies a crescent shaped bowl set amid thickly wooded hills at the upper end of Oslofjord. There are also numerous small islands within the fjord that belong to the city. Surrounding Oslo, the countryside is gently rolling and dotted with many fresh water lakes set amid mixed forests of broadleaf deciduous trees and conifers. Oslo is a picturesque, spotlessly clean yet modern city, reflecting both the past and forward look of the Norwegian people. Oslo has a population of only 560,000 and with its suburbs, it contain just over 1,000,000 people, but the city gives the appearance of being a large town rather than a major city. The heart of Oslo hugs the shoreline at the top of the fjord, surrounded by spacious suburbs that extend into the surrounding hills and along both shorelines of the fjord. There are now a few high-rise buildings along the waterfront and in the newer east end of the city center. The city also possesses a myriad of parks and gardens, all combining to give Oslo the feeling of being far less urbanized than it truly is. Unlike Stockholm or Copenhagen, there are more single-family houses in Oslo than the other two larger capitals. The majority of the houses in Oslo, and for that matter in all of Norway, are constructed of wood siding, generally painted white. A front porch is commonplace and the houses are set in small, but impeccably landscaped lots that show how much Norwegians care about their homes. And it is this flavor rather than the proliferation of apartment blocks that lends the aura of being in a small city rather than a major capital. This illusion is especially noticeable after first visiting Copenhagen or Stockholm where the apartment block predominates.

THE HISTORY OF OSLO: Oslo's heritage is that of the Vikings. Archaeological evidence shows that there were inhabitants in the area well before the end of the first millennium, yet Norse legend tells of the city having been founded in 1048 by King Harald Hardråe as a local trade center. So suffice it to say that Oslo is an old city. In 1261, King Håkon IV brought Norway to its golden age, forming a union with Iceland and Greenland. Oslo did not become the capital of the kingdom until the reign of King Håkon V (1299-1319). He is known to have been the first king to have actually taken up residence in the city, which was initially known as Christiana, later spelled Kristiana. The name was not changed to Oslo until 1925. To this day, the meaning of the name is unclear. It has been used as a boy's name but there is no single definition to its meaning. Several sources do say that it is taken from ancient Norse, and possibly means the meadow of the gods.

As Oslo grew in importance, its deep-water port closer to the interior heartland of the country with easier access first by road and later by rail slowly took away Bergen's significance as a port.

By the 14th century, Norway would be drawn into the Kalmar Union by Denmark. And in 1814, Norway became tributary to Sweden until 1905, thus the political significance of Oslo was far less important than that of Copenhagen or Stockholm. And this shows in the lack of many great stately buildings such as those found in the other two major Scandinavian capitals. The city was also primarily constructed of wood rather than stone or brick and it suffered numerous fires. The great 1624 fire actually caused the city to rebuild across the top end of the fjord where the city center is located today. The city rebuilt around Akershus Castle, which dates to the reign of King Haakon V who actually initially made Oslo the capital.

There is a less pretentious air about Oslo, as it still maintains its small city flavor. In 1814, when Norway once again became an independent kingdom in personal union with Sweden, the city began to take on more the feeling of an important center with the development of many public buildings, but to this day, it never lost its lack of pretention. The Royal Palace was built in 1848 and the Storting (national parliament) was built in 1866, the two most prominent buildings in the city center.

In 1952, Oslo played host to the winter Olympic games. These were the first post World War II winter games to be held. Norway was host to the 1994 winter Olympic games, held just north of Oslo in Lillehammer. This brought the focus of a lot of media attention to Oslo, as well as hundreds of thousands of visitors since the capital is also the major transport hub of the nation. Oslo was the city that Olympic athletes and visitors had to fly into, and then travel by train to Lillehammer. Despite its mountainous terrain, Norway does possess a significant railway system, and of course Oslo is the railroad hub of the country.

During World War II, Oslo became the seat of power for the puppet government under Nazi control. Freedom fighters were more active in sabotaging Nazi military installations rather than attacking many sites within the capital. But Nazi forces held a tight grip on the city, and its Jewish population, which was the largest in the country, was deported to concentration camps and few ever returned.

Since World War II, Norway has been considered one of the most peaceful and safest countries in Europe. But in summer 2011, a young Norwegian terrorist set off a large bomb in the government section of the city and then he opened fire on a group of young people at a summer camp on one of the islands in Oslofjord, killing 68 and wounding over 100. This was a catastrophic blow to national identity, as something like this could never have been anticipated in Norway.

VISITING THE CITY OF OSLO: When cruise ships are in port, their shore arrangements include city tours of Oslo, visiting many of the highlights. But if you choose to see the city on your own, you will find that public transport is quite good. Within the central part of the city there are numerous tramlines, and conductors can easily direct you to where you want to go since English is widely spoken. There is also an extensive commuter rail network that you can utilize to visit those few important venues that are out beyond the central city, especially the major Olympic ski jump facility in the hills above the city.

Although Oslo is a comparatively small city as seen on the map at the end of this chapter. It is filled with wonderful museums, galleries and parks. Being compact makes getting around easier than in some of the larger cities of the Baltic Sea region. Most of the city's main attractions are close to the waterfront around which the central downtown is built. Many of the important landmarks of Oslo include:
*Aker Brygge – the city's main central square, which faces the quay and the busy harbor. The way Oslo's downtown area radiates out from the harbor; it shows the importance of the docks to the city's overall economic well-being. Today many modern apartment and condominium blocks have spread out along the waterfront from the main square. There are also many restaurants and bistros making this a very lively district at night. It has become very

popular both with locals and visitors alike.

*Rådhus – the brick city hall, which dominates the heart of Oslo. Red brick is a popular building material throughout Scandinavia, since quarried stone is difficult to obtain.

*Stortorvet – the city's bustling market area, offering the visitor a glimpse into the rich diversity of seafood and produce.

*The Domkirke – the major cathedral of Oslo. Like all of Scandinavia, Norway is a strictly Protestant country, primary Lutheran.

*Akershus – the great fortress palace that once defended Oslo. It dates to the days when warfare was a major fact of life. Most cruise ships dock along the waterfront right at the base of the fortress, making it an easy venue to visit either at the start or end of the day's activities.

*The Royal Palace – home to the King of Norway. There is a changing of the guard at midday and the palace gardens are open to the public.

*Trivann's Tower – an observation tower to view the city if it is a clear day.

*The peninsula of Bygdøy - site of the most fashionable residences of Oslo. If you are on your own, I suggest simply walking around and just soaking in the atmosphere.

*Vigeland Sculpture Park – one of the city's major attractions with outdoor sculpture set amid lush greenery. Also known as Frognerparken, this massive park features hundreds of dramatic statues created by the master sculptor Gustav Vigeland. His view of mankind and its place in the world is quite distinctive and has won acclaim from art critics everywhere. The human figures depicted tell Vigeland's story of mankind, and you will either find that you can relate to his message or that you find it to be rather morose. There is little middle ground when it comes to the Vigeland Sculpture Park and how people react to it.

*Vigeland Museum - Adjacent to the park, this museum contains many of Vigeland's drawings and some of his marble sculptures.

*Fram Polar Ship Museum - This museum contains a major ice breaking exploration vessel and exhibits honoring Norway's polar explorations.

*Viking Ship Museum - This may be a small museum, but it does have several well preserved examples of early Viking ships and other artifacts to help explain these energetic explorers.

*Kon Tiki Museum - Dedicated to the famous anthropologist Thor Heyerdahl, this museum features vessels from his famous expedition in 1947. More on this important expedition is noted at the end of the list of attractions in Oslo.

*Holmenkollen Ski Jump and Museum - Located in the hills above the city, accessed by train from the city's main station, this is a must see venue. The Olympic ski jump itself is dramatic to view from up close. On a clear day, the view from Holmenkollen is magnificent.

*National Museum and National Gallery - Here you will find a good assortment of exhibits on Norwegian culture and art. Among the works of art is the world famous, but controversial painting by Edvard Munch entitled "The Scream.

*The Museum of Norwegian Resistance - For anyone with an interest in the role of the underground opposition to Nazi rule during World War II, this museum should be on your list. It is not well known, but it does document the role of the resistance fighters.

*The Norwegian Folk Museum - Here you can learn about the folk culture and arts and crafts of the Norwegian people. Much of the museum is open air and gives you the feel of walking through a traditional village.

*Karl Johan Gate - This grand boulevard runs from the heart of the city's shopping district past the Norwegian Parliament to Oslo University and the Royal Palace. The park along the west side of the street has a large outdoor cafe that is a popular spot for a cold drink or snack.

As you can see, Oslo is a city of museums. There is something for almost every taste, and I have not identified all of the museums. For those who have an interest in archaeology and anthropology or have wondered about the role of human migrations, a visit to the Kon Tiki Museum enables you to see Thor Heyerdahl's original raft, the Kon Tiki, that he sailed from Peru to French Polynesia in the mid 1900's. Heyerdahl was also the one who built a reed boat called the Ra'a, and he sailed it from the mouth of the Nile River to Central America, attempting to show a connection between ancient Egypt and the Maya. He is considered to have been Norway's premier anthropologist, and although his views have met with skepticism among many in his discipline, his adventurous spirit has never been doubted by any of his colleagues around the world. Even at present, there are those who dismiss him as simply an adventurer while others praise his work as a breakthrough in understanding how cultural traits may have been diffused between far distant locations.

MAXIMIZING YOUR TIME: After looking at the list of Oslo sights, you may ask how it is possible to see a large number of the venues described and also get a feel for the city of Oslo. Frankly it is impossible. Cruise ships stay for a maximum of a full day, but clearly it is insufficient time to see more than a handful of sights. Many cruise lines offer an overview tour of the city, but I personally find these tours to be very superficial. They attempt to provide a driving excursion through the city with few opportunities to stop at take photos or absorb what you are seeing. These tours will include from one to possibly three major venues where you will be herded through rather rapidly. If you are not the adventurous type or have physical disabilities, yes these tours are the best option for seeing Oslo or any of the cities on your itinerary. As a geographer, I favor personal exploration by one of the following means:

*Hiring a car and driver for the day, either through the cruise line or arranged by your travel agency. This gives you the freedom and flexibility to see the city on your terms, visiting the types of venues that suit your taste. This is a rather expensive way to visit any city, especially those in Scandinavia, but it does maximize your time.

*Hiring a taxi from the dock area is a less expensive way to have a personalized tour. In most Baltic Sea countries, you will find drivers who speak sufficient English or other languages to facilitate this type of exploration. Be sure to negotiate the price in advance as well as the method of payment.

*Utilizing local transportation can be challenging for most, but it is the more affordable way to get around on your own. Most city transport systems offer all day visitor passes. With a good map, some pre planning and patience, you can get around and have a rewarding day. Oslo does offer a good mix of trams, busses and a commuter rail network that will get you to all of the venues on the list above.

*There are hop on hop off busses available in Oslo. The routes will include the major venues of the city and operators provide maps and narratives to help maximize your independent explorations.

I have not listed any specific itineraries because that is not the nature of this publication. This is not meant to be a spoon fed guidebook such as those you can find in most bookstores. These chapters are meant to give you an geographic and historic perspective on each port of call and to point out the options available for your short time ashore.

DINING IN OSLO: Norwegian cuisine is heavily oriented toward seafood. Atlantic salmon is one of the country's great delicacies. One distinct Norwegian treat is gravlax. It is salmon that has been rubbed with sugar and dill, giving it a very distinct flavor through the way it is cured. Also on the menu is herring, an essential staple in the Norwegian diet, as are the very crisp flat breads made from wheat flour. Gravlox and herring are often eaten on these flat breads, topped with a piece of cheese. Fiskeboller is my favorite hot entree. It is made with chopped fish bound together with egg and breadcrumbs and then poached in fish broth. Fiskeboller can be served either hot or chilled. One Norwegian food item that many of us from the ret of the world may find difficult to accept is whale meat. I have tasted it by accident as part of a traditional buffet. It was prepared similar to meatballs. But when I tasted it and discovered that it was whale, I could not bring myself to eat it on general principle in that I believe whales are too magnificent to be slaughtered for food. But I must admit from the one bite I inadvertently tasted, it was very tender and flavorful, so I can understand why it is a popular food item.

Essentially the much of the food of Norway is very similar to that of Sweden, but with a bit more emphasis placed upon seafood and of course the addition of whale meat. And as is true throughout Scandinavia, rich pastries and ice creams are a definite part of the Norwegian dessert menu.

I am only going to recommend a few dining establishments that specialize in traditional Norwegian cuisine based upon my personal experiences. My friends and relatives all chide me about being a food "snob." That may be true, but I simply like dining at restaurants that offer the very best in quality and service. And in foreign countries I like to find excellent restaurants that offer the taste of that country. For Oslo I have three recommendations:
*Hos Thea - one of the finest restaurants in Oslo, specializing in Scandinavian dishes as well as cuisine from other parts of northern Europe. Hos Thea is elegant and the service is impeccable. However, unless your ship is staying late you may not be able to dine here, as they are only open from 5 to 10 PM for dinner. Located at Gabelsgate 11 in central Oslo.
*Statholdergaarden - A restaurant with 200 years of history located in an old house with nearly 400 years of antiquity, the atmosphere is superb, romantic for those who have that taste in mind. And the food is outstanding; once again they specialize in Scandinavian cuisine. Located in the central city at Radhusgata 11, and only open from 6 PM to Midnight for dinner.
*Grand Hotel Oslo - truly a grand hotel in every way, this venerable establishment is the city's number one hotel and it offers several world-class restaurants. For those on a cruise that will not be staying through the evening, I recommend the Grand Cafe, which faces out onto Karl Johan Gate. You have your choice of menu service or a buffet of delicious and traditional open face sandwiches. And when it comes to dessert, they offer a fantastic dessert buffet that will delight any sweet tooth. The cafe serves lunch and dinner. For a more elegant atmosphere, try Palmen, the main dining room for lunch or dinner. The cuisine is Norwegian and based upon the freshest ingredients of the season. Lunch, afternoon tea and dinner are served. The Grand Hotel is located on Karl Johan Gate opposite Parliament.

SHOPPING IN OSLO: Oslo is an expensive city in which both to dine and shop. Norway has one of the world's highest standards of living and oil revenues have added to the overall expense of living in or touring the country. There are several shopping venues in Oslo, but North Americans in particular will find the costs quite high. Apart from the normal tourist kitsch, there are fine quality woolens, hand knitted sweaters and very excellent quality Scandinavian made clothing, but you will pay top dollar. When I first started to visit Scandinavia every summer, I did not pay much attention to shopping, as few men do. But one summer I noticed that in all the cities there were major

July sales. That year I bought several pair of Swedish and Danish made jeans and sport shirts. I was so pleased with the quality and style that now each summer when I am in Scandinavia, I make shopping for clothes a major activity. For men the Scandinavian brands such as Sand, Tiger, J. Lindberg and Johansen are outstanding and well worth the expense. Sorry I do not have any experience with women's clothing, but I have noticed that Scandinavian women always appear to be stylish and well dressed. I do know that Sand and J. Lindberg also produces a line of very stylish women's casual clothing. The major shopping venues are:

*Oslo City Shopping Center - located opposite the central railway station at Stenersgaten 1, this is a collection of fashionable, but pricey shops.

*Karl Johan Gate - the main shopping street, especially south of the Parliament, is where many of the finest shops in Oslo will be found.

*Glas Magasinet - the largest and oldest department store in central Oslo, this beautiful store offers a broad variety of merchandise. It also offers a department featuring traditional Norwegian handicrafts. It is located at Stortorvet 9 in the city center.

*Steen and Strøm Magasin - this is Oslo's other major department store that offers many fashionable Scandinavian brands for both men and women. It is located on Nedre Slottsgate 8 in the city center.

*Eger Karl Johan - a smaller, but very fashionable store offering primarily clothing and accessories with an emphasis upon Scandinavian brands. It is located right on Karl Johan Gate 23.

FINAL WORDS: Although Oslo is one of the smaller capitals of SCANDINAVIA, it is a city that is rich in history, strong on pride and especially beautiful in a rather laid back manner. There are no grand boulevards or imposing monumental buildings, as is true in Stockholm. What Oslo lacks in grandeur it makes up for in charm.

One of the many picturesque villages along Oslofjord leading to Oslo

Small ferryboats ply Oslofjorden to connect its many villages

A dramatic view over Oslo from Holmansbyen Lookout

A view of the Oslo skyline as the ship docks

The skyline of Pipervika just west of city center

The hills above Oslo and the Holmenkollen Ski Jump

Karl Johan Gate looking to the Royal Palace

The Grand Hotel on Karl Johan Gate

The main square in Stortingate

The Royal Palace of Norway

Henrikke Park along Karl Johan Gate

Frogner Park and the Vigeland Sculpture Gardens (Work of Nick from Bristol, CC BY SA 2.0, Wikimedia.org)

Part of the wall around medieval Akerhus Castle on the waterfront

An example of a typical small Norwegian wood house in Oslo

Poached salmon, boiled potatoes and cucumber salad at the Grand Hotel in Oslo

A portion of the dessert buffet at the Grand Hotel in Oslo

STAVANGER

The greater Stavanger region. (© OpenStreetMap contributors)

The city of Stavanger. (© OpenStreetMap contributors)

The city center of Stavanger. (© OpenStreetMap contributors)

THE CITY'S GEOGRAPHIC SITE: Stavanger is the fourth largest city in Norway with a current metropolitan population of approximately 300,000. Until recently, it was the third largest city in the country, but it has been slightly overtaken by the city of Trondheim, and their local residents are very proud of their new ranking much to the dismay of Stavanger residents.

The city is located on the west coast of Norway, facing to the storm prone North Sea in the southern part of the country. Stavanger sits on the more sheltered leeward side of a large peninsula that faces out into the North Sea. On the eastern side is the wide bay called Boknafjorden. This is essentially an outlet bay that was initially deepened by the coalescing of several smaller glaciers as they reached what was thousands of years back a lower sea level. The land is relatively low and gently rolling, the result more of glacial deposits rather than scour. And the region is also quite beautifully forested, the wooded areas interspersed with farmland that has been meticulously tended over the centuries. The magnificent fjord country that visitors expect to find in every port of call in Norway is found adjacent to Stavanger, but not in the immediate vicinity of the city.

The peninsula on which the city is built does have a somewhat hilly and rocky character, often typical of the mixed debris having been deposited during the periods of glaciation. There are also numerous offshore islands that represent portions of the mainland cut off by the coming together of many glaciers before reaching the sea.

The climate is typical of the maritime coast of all southern Norway. There are few winter days with temperatures below freezing, but rather hovering in the low ranges combined with much rainfall to create a chilly, rainy environment. Summers are very mild, and rainfall is also prevalent throughout the so-called warmer season. Yet surprisingly this is a productive region agriculturally because of the longer daylight hours combined with mild temperatures and plenty of precipitation. The southern coastal region is not known for many days when you will find blue skies and brilliant sunshine. But on those rare days, the landscape definitely has an added sparkle to it.

SETTLEMENT OF STAVANGER: The area around Stavanger has a long history of settlement even predating the history of the Vikings. There is actual evidence of the town dating back to the 11th century, having become an important market center and seat of church activity once Christianity was established in southern Norway.

The official date of founding is the year 1125 when the beautiful Stavanger Cathedral was completed and the first bishop came to serve the area. It remained an important center of religious administration until the Protestant Reformation. In the early years of the 17th century, the bishop relocated to Kristiansand, and Stavanger then came to rely upon its local market role combined with the addition of the herring fishing fleet by the 19th century.

During World War II, the airport at Stavanger was bombed early in the morning of April 9, 1940, destroying the small Norwegian air contingent based there to protect this coastal region of the country. Within hours the Germans landed troops and supplies, the start of making this an important base of operation because of its strategic position facing out to the major sea traffic lane north to Murmansk in the Soviet Union. One of the most distinctive aspects of the German occupation of Stavanger was that in 1945 after the surrender, German soldiers were required by Norway to remain and remove all of the thousands of landmines that had been laid during the war.

When the Norwegians began to exploit their offshore oil reserves in the 1960's, it was recognized that Stavanger had two advantages, namely its large and deep harbor and secondly its proximity to the developing oil reserves, which were west and southwest of the city. As oil exploration expanded, other centers such as Haugesund, Bergen and Kristiansund also became important service centers for the oil drilling platforms. But Stavanger was the first, and it is still vital to the petroleum production industry. However, the decline in oil prices and the essential overproduction has caused a major degree of disruption to the industry. This has also caused the population growth rate and the overall economic output of the city to stagnate.

THE CITY TODAY: Until recently, Stavanger was able to boast that it was the third largest city in Norway after Oslo and Bergen. It presently has a metropolitan area population of 319,000, but its city population is approximately 127,000. Trondheim is shown to have a city population of 176,000. But metropolitan Trondheim is still slightly below that of Stavanger according to most Norwegian sources.

As a visitor off of a cruise ship, there are many interesting sights in Stavanger, and of course most cruise lines have a variety of tours planned. I personally prefer to get out on my own, but that is because I have been to Norway around 20 times in the last ten years. If this is your first cruise through the fjords, then of course a tour in a small city like Stavanger will enable you to see all the major sights either in the city or the surrounding countryside, depending upon your preference.

As one of the oldest cities in Norway, there is a good degree of historic architecture, especially in the old town area. Although this was a well settled region during Viking times, as with all major Norwegian cities and towns, the emphasis architecturally is upon those elements of northern European tradition that were infused into the country with the coming of early Christian priests and merchant traders.

Stavanger sprawls along the water and into the hills behind the old city center. There is urban development on several of the small adjacent islands, connected to the central city by a network of small ferryboats. Most of Stavanger's residential districts are built of wood, a common building material in much of Norway because of the abundance of forests and the development of a forest industry. And the majority of the city's thousands of houses are painted white. Brick and stone tend to be reserved for public and commercial buildings rather than for individual homes.

Today there are many modern moderately tall apartment blocks lining the waterfront and the city center does possess a few contemporary skyscrapers, but nothing that would be exceptionally tall. Remember that this is a small urban center by overall European standards.

WHAT TO SEE AND DO IN STAVANGER: Here is my listing of the major sites worth your time while sightseeing within the city. And this is followed by the major locales outside of the city that can be visited within less than the usual six to eight hours that most cruise ships allow for Stavanger.

* Old Town Stavanger - The old sector of the city with its tightly packed whitewashed wood houses lining narrow streets so typifies the older cities found along the Atlantic coast of the country. There are also many small shops and restaurants that have opened in the old sector because this has become a focus of cruise tourism because of its proximity to the waterfront. Many of the streets are now reserved only for pedestrians, but some are rather steep since much of the Old Town climbs the adjacent hills, which typify so much of the urban landscape. There are many words to describe the old sector such as quaint, picturesque, romantic or even fairytale like. It does give you a good picture of what urban Norway was like even at the start of the 20th century.

* Skagenkaien - Here along the waterfront you will find much of the early maritime architecture of the city, dating back to the founding of the port. And like the Old Town area, you will find Skagenkaien heavily oriented toward serving the tourists, especially on days when ships are in port. This area is also very close to where cruise ships dock, so for those with limited mobility, this is the easiest venue to visit.

* Stavanger Cathedral - Located at the edge of a beautiful parkland just to the southwest of the city center, this cathedral began as a Catholic center for the regional bishop. After an 18th century fire, the restoration of the main facade changed the entire look of the building, as under Protestant domination it was given more simplified lines. Originally this cathedral was closely tied to southern England, as it was English priests that first came to Stavanger in the 16th century.

* Valbergtarnet - This is the old watchtower standing on a high hill just to the east of the city center. In the days before any form of telecommunication, this was how the city protected itself by having watchmen on shift to look for the start of fires or even for the threat of outside invasion. Today it offers an outstanding close in view of the city center, giving the visitor some excellent photographic opportunities.

* Stavanger Maritime Museum - Here you get a complete history with exhibits that relate Stavanger to the sea, and it is sure to please anyone who is interested in the role of sea commerce and the coast of Norway. It is located at the southern end of the old harbor at Strandkaien # 22 and also maintains limited hours from 11 AM to 4 PM daily. The museum does feature a good collection of replicas of small sailing vessels and early ships.

* Norwegian Canning Museum - This museum presents the history of fishing for commercial canning and its role in the development of Stavanger. It is located along the narrow old harbor just north of the Old Town area at Oevre Strabdgate #88. It has limited hours between 10 AM and 4 PM daily.

* Norwegian Petroleum Museum - I recommend this only for those who are truly interested in the industrial history of the city and the important role played by North Sea oil. Located on the waterfront in the main dock area at Kjeringholmen # 1-a, it provides an insight into the oil and natural gas industry and what it means to Stavanger. Surprisingly, most visitors who are skeptical about visiting such a specific museum actually come away quite pleased that they visited.

* Swords in the Rock is an important monument to Norway's early history. It is located at Hafrsfjord on the southwestern edge of the city. Without this being part of a tour, you will need to either have a private car or commission a local taxi on an hourly rate to get here. Or if you would like to try local transportation, city bus number 29 will bring you here from the city center. The monument consists of three hilts of old Viking swords that protrude from solid rock in the same fashion as the famous Excalibur in the King Arthur legends. The monument celebrates a great battle fought in 872 in which Harald Harfagre was victorious and united most of the Viking tribes of Norway into a single nation.

* The Museum of Archaeology is located southwest of the city center, actually not too far south of the Cathedral. It is at Pedre Klowsgate #30-A and is also open only from 11 AM to 3 PM. Here you will find a good collection of artifacts and exhibits that portray the end of the glacial era along with the earliest evidence of human occupancy prior to the Viking culture. The museum also has a small cafe for quick meals.

For those who want to explore some of the natural beauty of the countryside outside of Stavanger, there are a few locations that you can get to either as part of a ship sponsored tour or on your own with a private car or taxi. My recommendations are:

* Lysefjorden - If your cruise line offers a boat trip into Lysefjorden and if you want to truly see some magnificent scenery, then this is an option I would highly recommend. This narrow fjord located across the broad bay known, as Boknafjorden is a short distance from the city, yet it is a world away, as the fjord is narrow and the walls are steep, offering some beautiful photo opportunities.

* Vaulen Beach - Located just south of the city on the east side of the peninsula, Vaulen Beach is not quite the rugged out of door environment since it is still within the greater urban zone. But it does offer beautiful scenery of a rather placid nature, having calm waters, small groves of trees and

surrounded by low hills albeit there are still some houses in view. But it is a nice retreat from the heart of Stavanger and is easily accessed by private car or taxi.

DINING OUT: Depending upon your cruise company's itinerary you may or may not have time for lunch. Many people prefer to skip an actual restaurant lunch and simply have a quick snack so as to not loose time. But I personally think that the dining experience is part of the adventure. So if you want to enjoy a traditional Norwegian lunch, here are my choices:

* Fisketorget - Located in the city center at Strandkaien # 37 and open for lunch from 11 AM onward, it is my first choice for traditional Norwegian seafood dishes. Two of the most popular dishes are a hearty fish soup and then followed by cod that has been sautéed with bacon. If cod is not to your taste, there are also choices ranging from salmon to whatever is the freshest catch of the day.

* Sjohuset Skagen - This very traditional restaurant is located in the city center as well, its exact address being Skagenkaien #13. It is open from 11:30 AM onward and specializes in seafood, which is of course what one expects in Norway. Their fish soup is said by many to be the best in Stavanger, but of course you must be the judge. They also serve whale meat, a very traditional dish in Norway. I have tried it, and yes it has a wonderful taste, but somehow I could not bring myself to go beyond just a taste, knowing it was whale. But again that is a decision you must make.

* Det Lille Hjornet - Located in the city center at Overe Holmegate #29 and open from 11 AM onward, this is my recommendation for those of you who just want a quick soup or sandwich or simply a dessert and tea or coffee. This is informal and service is quick so you can be on your way again to see more of the city.

SHOPPING: Stavanger is not really a major shopping destination for cruise passengers, as it has primarily souvenir stores in the Old City. The most common item that people wish to buy is a hand knitted Norwegian sweater, and yes you will find a fair selection in the Old City area. But for a larger selection, I would recommend waiting until you get to Bergen unless you see something that you feel you absolutely must have.

FINAL WORDS: Stavanger is a beautiful city that typifies the gracious, yet not ostentatious lifestyle of the people of Norway. And as the country's third major urban region, it does offer all of the important services for its people and those in the hinterland. From a tourist perspective, there is a lot of historic architecture that will hold your interest.

A high altitude aerial over Stavanger looking to the southwest

An aerial over central Stavanger. (Work of Oyvind Rask, CC BY SA 4.0 Wikimedia.org)

Typical wood houses of Stavanger. (Work of Holger Uwe Schmitt, CC BY SA 4.0, Wikimedia.org)

The Stavanger waterfront. (Work of Holger Uwe Schmitt, CC BY SA 4.0, Wikimedia.org)

In the heart of the older commercial center of Stavanger. (Work of Christian Bickel, CC BY SA 2.0, Wikimedia.org)

The modern side of Stavanger's waterfront. (Work of Zairon, CC BY SA 3.0, Wikimedia.org)

The old waterfront market area. (Work of Ranveig, CC BY SA 1.0, Wikimedia.org)

One of Stavanger's beautiful public gardens. (Work of Kilabas, CC BY SA 4.0 International, Wikimedia.org)

HAUGESUND

The Haugesund region (© OpenStreetMap contributors)

Map of the inner city of Haugesund (© OpenStreetMap contributors)

LOCATION: Haugesund is located just north of Stavanger but not many cruise ships seem to pay a port call, which I think is a shame because it is a delightful small city with a picturesque setting, wonderful architecture and delightful people. If your itinerary is fortunate enough to include Haugesund, you will find it an enjoyable visit.

The city is actually in a very strategic location because it lies at the northern end of the Karmsundet, a rather narrow, but deep inside passage that begins across the opening of Boknafjorden. Once passing through this channel and passing Haugesund, ships need only be in the open sea for another short stretch before they can enter another inside passage all the way to Bergen. Given the severity of the winter weather on the North Sea and also the occasional summer storms that can bring rough seas, the inside passages along most of the Norwegian coast has been a safe haven for ships plying the waters north and south between such ports as Arkhangelsk and Murmansk on the Barents Sea in far northern Russia and the Baltic Sea, which is reached after rounding the southern tip of Norway and passing between Denmark and Sweden.

The region surrounding Haugesund both on the large islands and the mainland is gently rolling to moderately hilly. The land where not cleared for agriculture consists of thick coniferous forests and the countryside is dotted with hundreds of glacial lakes while the coastline is indented with several fjords, both signs of intense glaciation.

Climatically this area is within the maritime regime that dominates most of Norway until one gets beyond the Arctic Circle where a sub polar climatic regime begins. Winters are cold, hovering just around or above freezing and more rain than snow is commonplace. Thus blustery, damp and gray weather is the norm. Summers are very mild, and with the warm offshore Gulf Stream, fog is quite common as the moist air looses its ability to hold the vapor, condensing it out into microscopic droplets suspended above ground level. The last time I visited Haugesund in 2015, it was a mild, almost warm, August day with blue skies, but by mid afternoon a bank of fog came in from the open sea and visibility was reduced to almost zero in a matter of minutes.

Haugesund is an important regional center for the surrounding farmland, fishing, servicing oil drilling platforms and fjord tourism. It is a very pleasant city with a population of 40,150 in its metropolitan area. The city presents both the feel of a small town, yet it has all of the important amenities of a city, including a well developed business district, a beautiful cathedral, public buildings and parks. Like so many Norwegian cities, it is built on a series of hills, rising back from the waterfront and consists primarily of wood houses, most of them painted white. Public buildings are constructed of brick or stone, and many date to the late 18th and 19th centuries.

BRIEF HAUGESUND HISTORY: Like so much of southern Norway, archaeological evidence shows that there have been settlements in the region for many thousands of years, dating back to around 6,000 years ago. By the time of the Viking Era, starting in the 10th century, this was an important area for trade, including contacts across the North Sea to the British Isles.

The region is known as Rogaland, and it was an important Viking stronghold. A great battle for control of Rogaland took place in 872 when King Harald Fairhair was victorious and incorporated the area into his expanding Norwegian kingdom. The actual details of this victory are told in the Norwegian Sagas and some say they are as much myth as reality, somewhat like the stories of King Arthur and Camelot. A great monument, known as Haraldshaugen, was built in 1872 to commemorate the 1,000 anniversary of the great battle outside of Haugesund to honor King Harald, as the greatest early king of Norway. It is believed to be on the site where his burial mound exists.

During much of its history, the fishing for herring dominated the local economy, but the stocks have been so badly depleted that they have not been viable since the early years of the 20th century. But since the mid 1960's, Haugesund, like Stavanger, has become a major center for servicing the oil drilling platforms off shore in the North Sea.

SIGHTSEEING DURING YOUR PORT CALL: Many cruise lines choose to bypass Haugesund, especially if they stop in Stavanger because the two cities are so close to one another. But if you are fortunate enough to visit Haugesund, it most likely will be a short port call, either a few hours in the morning or afternoon, as rarely do any cruise ships spend an entire day. As usual, you can take a group tour around the city, but for those of you who want to go off on your own, here are my recommendations of places you really should see:
* Haraldshaugen - This is the most recognized major site to visit within Haugesund. It is located just north of the city and can be reached by private car or local taxi. You can also walk, as it is only two kilometers from the city center. Built in 1872, it commemorates the 1,000th anniversary of the famous battle fought in this area that ultimately unified southern Norway under the Viking King Harald Fairhair. He is also believed to be buried here according to the Norwegian Sagas.

* Haraldsgata is the main pedestrian shopping street, and it gives you a good look at the basic lifestyle of the city

Our Savior's Church dominates the skyline of the city center with its tall, red tower. The architectural style is very typical of 18th or 19th century churches in small Norwegian cities. And the landscaped grounds surrounding the church offer a quiet refuge

*Haugesund Town Hall is one of the most beautiful public buildings along the southern coast of Norway. Given as a gift by a wealthy ship owner, it only dates to 1931, yet it has become recognized as an architectural masterpiece throughout the country

* Arquebus War History Museum is located at the top end of Førrestfjorden about 30 kilometers from Haugesund. This is one of those special locations that requires either a private car or taxi unless it happens to be part of a shi's tour. The museum is housed in a former German bunker, and is one of the best in Norway for telling the history of the Nazi occupation during WWII. The museum is open daily from 11 AM t0 5 PM during the summer season.

* Djupadalan is an outdoor wooded area set aside for public hiking and recreation. If you are an outdoor type and would like to spend a few hours trekking through the woods on a well marked path, this is the place to visit. It is located about eight kilometers east of the town center in the foothills and can be reached by private car or local taxi. This is a delightful walk that is suitable for all ages, and bicyclists often use this route, with bicycle rentals available in the city center.

* Steinsfjellet - Located about 20 kilometers east of the city at an altitude of 227 meters or 744 feet above sea level, this observation point gives you a grand view of the city, surrounding woods, small lakes and the shoreline. The drive is rather pleasant, but being outside of the city, you need to have arranged for a private car or hire a local taxi.

DINING OUT: Unless your port call is for an entire day, you will either leave before the lunch hour or arrive afterwards. But for those who can spend an entire day in Haugesund, or for those who want a quick snack, I am providing my recommendations for one traditional Norwegian restaurant and one cafe that offers light snacks.

* Brasserie Brakstad - Located in the city center at Kaigata #2 and open from 11 AM onward, this restaurant offers a casual atmosphere. The menu features a wide variety of Norwegian and general Scandinavian dishes featuring both seafood and meat entrees.

* Naturbaskt - Located at Haraldsgata and Skippergaten, and open from & AM onward, this is an ideal bakery/cafe where you can get a variety of sandwiches, soups and typical Norwegian pastries. This is my recommendation for a cafe that offers quick service and light meals.

FINAL WORDS: If you visit Haugesund and you are fortunate enough to have clear, sunny weather, you will find this a delightful community. But as noted earlier, weather plays a major role and when it is foggy there is less likelihood that you will dock if scheduled to do so. But when you are able to visit, Haugesund, though nothing special, is just an enjoyable place in which to savor a bit of small city life Norwegian style.

Flying over Haugesund, looking southwest (Work of Sjakkalle, CC BY SA 4,0, Wikimedia.org)

Looking north along the main channel through Haugesund

Looking south along the main channel through Haugesund

Risøybrua over the main channel connecting Risøy Island to town center

Strandgata is the main shopping street of Haugesund

Our Savior's Cathedral in the heart of Haugesund

Typical white painted wood houses of Haugesund

An oil drilling platform being built in Haugesund

BERGEN
NORWAY'S SECOND CITY

Map of Greater Bergen (© OpenStreetMap contributors)

Map of the city of Bergen (© OpenStreetMap contributors)

Bergen is the second largest city in Norway and for many cruise itineraries through the fjord country, it is the largest city that the ship will visit since few such cruises begin or end in Oslo. Today Bergen's population, including all of its outlying suburban reaches, is approximately 420,000. The city does not seem that large because of its physical geography. The first map in this chapter makes it easy to understand how the perception of size is affected by the urban layout. The city center is found on a small peninsula formed by two deep water inlets, giving the city two distinct harbors. Mt. Fløyen rises up to the north of the main harbor, rising to an elevation of 987 meters or 3,238 feet. The bulk of the city stretches from the city center southward in a narrow valley that is formed between two parallel mountain ridges. There are also urbanized areas along the northern shore underneath Mt. Fløyen and wrapping around the mountainous peninsula that separate the southern residential core from the main channel. Suburbs also spill out onto the large islands that protect the city from the full force of North Sea winters.

This complex geographic interrelationship between land and water is again the result of glacial scour. Numerous tongues of glacial ice swept down former river valleys between the mountain spurs and their forward edges coalesced when they reached the sea, which at that time was much lower than today. After retreating the sea rose and it flooded these now deepened channels, creating the complex network of fjords, islands and deep water channels between the mainland those pieces of land that now form the complex strings of islands along Norway's coast. Many small scoured basins amid the mountains filled with melt water and today comprise the thousands of glacial lakes that pepper the landscape.

The entire region is cloaked in thick coniferous forest, its growth heightened by the heavy precipitation that results from mild, moist air being forced to rise along the mountainous coast. This maritime climate begins to change in the vicinity of Bergen, as the more northerly latitude equates to shorter winter days, which end up being colder and thus snowfall down to sea level is more common that farther south at Stavanger. Summers are mild with daytime temperatures rarely climbing above the upper 70's or mid 20's C. Gray overcast and fog are commonplace, and Bergen is said to be the least sunny major city in Norway. With climatic changes, rainfall in Bergen has increased and today averages close to 90 inches (2,280 millimeters) per year. The city actually announces in its tourist brochures that it is the rainiest city in the country and chides itself in not having a sunnier climate. Thus when you visit Bergen you should not expect blue skies and sunshine, although during July and August there can be several consecutive days with absolutely beautiful weather that makes the city so amazingly photogenic. In my photos at the end of this chapter, I have chosen from among my best taken over the past ten years of multiple visits. Perhaps that is not fair to those of you reading this book, as it gives a false illusion of Bergen's true weather. But at least knowing is being prepared. Bring an umbrella and a raincoat.

BERGEN 'S HISTORY: There is a bit of rivalry between the residents of Bergen and those of Oslo. Both cities date to within a few years of one another, so they are each among the oldest cities in Norway. But Bergen was the capital and most important city of Norway during its early years as a unified nation until the year until some time during the reign of King Hakon V who moved the capital to Oslo some time after 1299. Thus Bergen residents take pride in their early royal history while Oslo residents take pride in the fact that their city is now the capital and also the largest city of the nation.

The Bergen Domkyrken (cathedral0 was built in 1150 and was the site of royal functions such as coronations, marriages and burials all through the rest of the 12th and 13th centuries. During its latter part of its time as the early capital, the Bergenhus Fortress, which stands watch over the northern harbor, served as a royal residence. During the 14th century, despite having lost the capital to Oslo, Bergen was a minor trade center under the Hanseatic League, but the surviving architecture along the waterfront of Bryggen lacks the distinctive ornamentation of traditional Hanseatic buildings. However, their unique character and wood construction has merited UNESCO World Heritage status.

Bergen grew both as a port, but also as a major center for the catching of cod and the drying of the fish for export. The trade became so lucrative that if any other city wanted to develop its own cod fishing/drying enterprise, it first had to obtain permission of the king.

Despite its loss of the capital, Bergen was still a major Scandinavian city, and actually was larger than Oslo until almost the mid 19th century. It suffered the bubonic plague in the mid 14th century, was attacked by pirates in the 15th century and by a British naval fleet that was after a Dutch treasure fleet under city protection in 1655.

Like Oslo, Bergen also suffered from the ravages of fire because of the persistent use of wood as the primary building material. Various parts of the city experienced massive burning during every century until the mid 20th century. Today that danger still exits in Bryggen and other older neighborhoods where wood houses are clustered together along narrow streets that often are very steep where parts of the city climb the surrounding hills.

Bergen was among the first cities in Norway to be attacked and then occupied by Nazi forces during April 1940. Because of its port facilities, it became an important German naval facility and was subjected to bombing by Allied forces. Given its strategic location along the major shipping lane for the Allies in their aid of the Soviet Union, Bergen was of prime value to the German navy.

In the late 20th century the cruise industry discovered the Norwegian fjords, and ever since Bergen has been the major urban stop on almost all itineraries. During a typical summer day there can be three to four major cruise ships anchored in Bergen, generating thousands of visitors and significant revenue for the city's merchants and tour operators.

VISITING BERGEN: Most cruise passengers opt for one of the ship's tours when visiting Bergen simply because it is a large, spread out city. A tour maximizes your time and enables you to see more of the major sights. A less expensive, but not as good an option is the hop on hop off bus, and there is almost always one waiting in front of the cruise dock. Of course my preferred option is to have a private car and driver when it comes to a city this size. You can explore on foot or combine walking with public transport, but it will be far more time consuming and at the end of the day you will be exhausted.

My recommendation for the must see sights in Bergen includes:
* Mt. Fløyen - This is the number one tourist venue on anyone's list of places to see in Bergen. But there is one caveat - The weather must be good. Mt. Fløyen is reached by a funicular whose base is opposite the famous fish market at the upper end of the north harbor. The funicular will take you up to the observation level atop the mountain, 320 meters or 1,049 feet above sea level for a very dramatic view over the entire city and its surrounding mountains, water and islands. All of Bergen will be at your feet, but only if it is a blue sky day or if scattered clouds are above the level of the surrounding mountains. If you are going on your own, I recommend as early in the day as possible because the crowds gather soon after 9 AM and the wait can be well over an hour, but it is worth the wait. If you are on a tour, your group will get special preference. There is a teahouse and gift shop along with walking trails on top of the mountain.
* Historic Bryggen - Here along the waterfront you will find the oldest surviving wood buildings in the city. Bryggen was once the center of the Hanseatic merchant's quarter and dates back to the 14th and 15th century. Many of the buildings today house fine arts and crafts shops, cafes and

restaurants. This is the most popular part of the city center and is often crowded when two or more ships are in port.

* Bryggens Museum - This small museum located in the old city district of Bryggen at Dreggsallmenningen # 3 and open daily from 10 AM to 4 PM presents a good look at life in Bergen in the days of the city's early development through the Hanseatic period.

* Bergen Fish Market - Red is the color that best describes the Fish Market, located at the upper end of the north harbor, opposite Bryggen and at the start of the city's main shopping street, which is Torgallmenningen. Between the displays of fresh salmon, cooked crab and shrimp and the magnificent strawberries and raspberries, red dominates the Fish Market. Jars of primarily salmon caviar are also available and make a popular souvenir item to take home. There are vendors selling cooked or smoked fish ready to eat on the spot or hot fish soup. But most visitors come just to look and photograph the displays of seafood and berries. If you happen to see a dark reddish brown meat that looks more like fresh beef liver, it is not. It is whale meat, as Norway and Japan are two nations where whale meat is still considered a delicacy and neither country will sign onto a moratorium on whaling. At times Green Peace protestors have come to Bergen and other Norwegian ports to garner public support, but so far to no avail.

* St. Mary's Church - This beautiful Romanesque building dates back to the 12th century when Bergen was the first capital of a united Norway. It is where early Norwegian kings had their coronations, weddings and funerals. Located at Dreggen # 15 it is easy to spot from a distance by looking for its twin bell towers.

* Troldhaugen - This is the small house and estate that was home to Norway's most celebrated classical composer, Edvard Grieg. It is a museum dedicated to the famous composer and somewhat of a shrine to those familiar with the composer's music. Open daily from 9 AM to 6 PM, it is often offered as a special ship's tour on various cruise lines. If you go on your own and do not have a car, take the light rail from the city center at Festplassen and get off at Hop Station then follow the signs.

* Rosenkrantz Tower - Often called the Bergen Castle or Fortress, it was begun in 1270 but not completed until 1560. It served as both a royal residence and a watchtower because of its position on the northern harbor. It is also part of the overall fortress defenses that once protected the city.

* Fantoft Stavkirke - Here is one of the classic examples of the old Norwegian rural stave churches, built entirely out of wood and once commonplace around the country. This church is now in the southern suburbs and is often included on organized tours of the city. If you are on your own, you can reach it via the light rail by boarding at the Festplassen where the light rail begins or ends in

the city center. Take the train south to the Paradis Station and follow the signs.

* KODE - The Art Museum of Bergen located along the southeastern edge of Festplassen, it is a significant art museum featuring many works by famous Scandinavian artists. It is open daily from 10 AM to 5 PM.

DINING OUT: Most cruise itineraries allow a full day and often much of the evening in Bergen. With the great variety of restaurants located in the city center, which is a short walk from where cruise ships dock, I highly recommend either lunch or dinner in the city. Here is a chance to enjoy great Norwegian food with a heavy emphasis upon fresh seafood. I have several restaurant recommendations primarily for lunch, and in each case I have chosen a venue that specializes in traditional Norwegian cuisine.

* Bare Vestland is a traditional Norwegian restaurant that specializes in both seafood and meats prepared in the western Norwegian tradition. Their menu is very diverse and there will be a dish or two to please any taste, and they also have a broad selection of beers. Open daily from Noon onward and located close to the Fish Market at Vaagsallmenningen #2, this is a place that many locals patronize, so it is not strictly for tourists.

* Bryggeloftet & Steuene is a major restaurant on the waterfront in Bryggen. You cannot miss it because of its large marquee at the front. It is also in a prominent multi story brick building, which is not a common sight in Bergen. Open daily from 11:30 AM, you will find a very diverse menu, but the emphasis is upon seafood. And one of its specialties is a delicious fish soup, a Norwegian tradition. This is a top choice for either lunch or dinner and it is only about a 15 minute walk from where most ships dock.

* Restaurant Cornelius - If you want to escape the city and the hoards of tourists, have the ship make a lunch or dinner reservation at this restaurant located on the island of Byorøya south of the city center in the main fjord along which the city is built. You will be given instructions as to where to meet their private boat that will take you to the restaurant and return you to the city. Here you will enjoy a fantastic seafood dinner pared with great wines in a setting that is idyllic and if the weather is nice, you can eat outside on their deck overlooking the water. They open at noon daily, but a reservation is necessary since they must arrange transportation.

* Fjellskal Fisketorget - Located on the waterfront just to the south and west of the Fish Market at Strandkalen #3, this is one of the city's most noted seafood restaurants. Opening at 8 AM, it remains open way into the night, serving both lunch and dinner. The array of fish and shellfish dishes is quite amazing, as are the fish soups. Freshness is the hallmark along with excellent preparation. And you are directly on the water where fishing boats are docking to unload their catch.

* Krok og Krinkle Bokcafe - If dessert is all you crave, this is the place to come, as it is considered the number one cafe for typical Norwegian pastries. Located at Lille Oevregaten # 14 just up hill from the Fish Market and open from 9 AM to 7 PM, you can enjoy a light breakfast, coffee or pastry in a relaxed atmosphere among shelves of books and antique furniture pieces. It is the type of cafe where people choose to linger.

SHOPPING: As a major city and also a center for tourism, there are many good shopping venues in Bergen, but only one that I felt was significant in its uniqueness. In addition, I note the downtown mall, but it does not measure up to what you would find in Oslo or other major Scandinavian cities. There are many small shops in Bryggen that sell the typical souvenirs and also the hand knitted Norwegian sweaters. But frankly none stand out as very unique. And you will find the same types of gift items, sweaters and kitsch all throughout your cruise. It is just that Bergen has a larger selection.
* Galleriet - This is the largest shopping mall in the city center, located at Torgallmenningen # 8 in the heart of the downtown. It contains a variety of shops and cafes on several levels, but it is nothing out of the ordinary if you have previously shopped in other major cities. But it does offer all of the basics, and when it comes to men's and women's casual clothing there are several Norwegian brands that are of good quality at reasonable prices.
* Julehuset Christmas Shop is a place where you can celebrate Christmas all year. It is located in Bryggen at Holmedalsgaarden #1 and open from 10 AM to 6 PM daily. On three floors you will find a wide array of souvenir items along with traditional Norwegian Christmas decorations and tree ornaments.
*
FINAL COMMENTS: Over the years I have traveled through Norway, I have been to Bergen at least a dozen times. I always enjoy the overall flavor of the city, appreciating its antiquity mixed with modernity. It is exceptionally fresh and clean and has essentially an unhurried feeling even though thousands of tourists crowd into Bryggen and the Fish Market area. But you can take many quiet walks through its older residential areas, or ride the light rail out to quiet, leafy suburbs and come to understand what it is like to live in this coastal city. The only real drawback can be the weather, which is so hard to predict. One never knows if it will be a rainy day, just overcast or if you will have blue skies. In July and August you will find the greatest chance of experiencing nice weather in Bergen. But please do not let the weather limit your getting out and experiencing the city. Umbrellas should always be at hand.

The inner city of Bergen (© OpenStreetMap contributors)

The city center from atop Mt. Fløyen

A view from Mt. Fløyen looking to the left of the prior view

The skyline of the old city quarter north of the Fortress

On the back streets of Bryggen, the old city quarter

The colorful displays of salmon and other seafood in the Fish Market

Fresh strawberries and raspberries in the Fish Market

In the heart of the city's main shopping district

The famous gazebo in Festplassen in the city center

The man made lake and fountain in Festplassen

The light rail that begins or ends at Festplassen

On the back streets of old Bergen just north of the city center

The city center peninsula seen from on board ship in the northern harbor

Beautiful single family homes on the outer islands west of the city center

Two major suspension bridges help connect the islands with the city center

Old 19th century houses show that the islands have been long a part of the city

SOGNEFJORD
VISITING FLÄM AND GUDVANGEN

Sognefjord country, Fläm is the right hand star (© OpenStreetMap contributors)

Visiting Fläm and Gudvangen is often the highlight of those cruises that are not going all the way north into Arctic Norway. It is very difficult to say which fjord system is the most beautiful. I have my favorites based upon their photogenic attributes, but in essence every fjord in Norway is special. And the Sognefjord system with its two major stops of Fläm and Gudvangen is hard to duplicate. Depending upon the amount of cloud cover vs. sunlight, the dappling of the landscape while sailing into these two small villages can simply be magical. There is no other word that seems to describe it.

Remember that fjords are the result of pre glacial river systems having been scoured by glacial ice, often widened and definitely deepened most often with sheer vertical walls. Every major fjord thus has tributary smaller fjords, presenting a rather complex landscape that can extend over 100 kilometers from the upper reaches to the sea. As tiny creeks converge together and then form the major pre glacial river system, they generally plunge directly down into the now deepened gorges, creating what amounts to hundreds of waterfalls. And given Norway's northern latitude and the altitude of its mountains, small glaciers still exist in the highest peaks and snow lingers along the tops of the fjords well into the summer, thus providing for sufficient water to keep the falls in full form. The two major southern branches of Sognefjord are Aurlandsfjorden, which is the location for the village of Fläm and Nærøyfjord, home to the village of Gudvangen.

THE PORT OF FLÄM: Normally most cruise itineraries call for an early morning entry into Sognefjord, cruising slowly inbound for at least four to five hours before reaching Aurlandsfjorden, which is rather of short length. The journey is quite spectacular in the early morning light, of course providing the weather is relatively good. the best conditions are those when the sky is clear and there is a small amount of ground fog or mist swirling around the steep cliffs. I find that most often you can count the number of guests out on deck on one hand, as the majority are either sleeping or preparing for the day's activities. To experience the beauties of Sognefjord, one must normally be out on deck at around 5:30 AM. But there is still an opportunity to enjoy a different perspective during the evening sail out from Gudvangen, as most ships will not reach the open sea until approximately 10 PM.

Arrival at Fläm is generally in the morning at around 8 or 9 AM. There is a single small dock that is capable of handling one medium size cruise ship, and it is available on a first come basis whenever the local car ferries are not arriving at the same time. In the event the dock is occupied by a ferry or an earlier ship then your ship will drop anchor in the fjord and you will tender to and from shore by means of one of the ship's lifeboats. The only disadvantage is that such transfers can add up to half an hour to the time going to or coming from shore.

Fläm is the coastal terminus of the Flämsbana, a railroad link of approximately 20.2 kilometers or 12.6 miles, but rising 867 meters or 2,844 feet in elevation. It connects Aurlansfjorden with the main railway line that links Oslo with Bergen. This train journey, which takes a little more than an hour each way, is the highlight of the day for most guests. It is one of the world's most spectacular rail journeys with a constantly changing panorama of the glacial valley, mountain peaks and a myriad of waterfalls. To accomplish the construction, the line is a single track standard gauge with corresponding overhead electric cables to provide power. There are 18 tunnels on the line, which has an average 2.8 percent grade.

Depending upon your cruise line's various options, you can either ride the train all the way to Myrdal where it connects with the main line and then return, a total journey time of approximately two hours. Some cruise lines offer a stop at Vatnahalsen where you have an hour before taking the return train. And most stops include waffles and coffee at the Vatnahalsen Inn. The longest option offered by some cruise itineraries has guests transferring to the main line train destined for Voss, located a short distance to the west. At Voss, guests board a motor coach for a dramatic journey back down the mountains, but to Gudvangen where they meet the ship later in the afternoon. And this option includes a lunch break along with many scenic stops.

For those who remain in Fläm, usually only a handful of guests, there is very little to do. Fläm is a village with a handful of shops, a nice hotel and a few dozen private residences. There are a few walking paths, but the time will pass slowly since the stop is around four hours duration and after an hour there will be nothing more to see or do.

THE PORT OF GUDVANGEN: It will take your ship about two hours to sail back down Aurlandsfjorden and into Nærøyfjord and the small village of Gudvangen. This is accomplished at midday, and on those days when it is sunny or even just partly cloudy, the voyage is nothing less than spectacular. Most guests will crowd into the ship's observation lounges or be out on deck to absorb the raw beauty of this transfer between the two fjords. I have done this trip at least a dozen times, and each time is like the first. The sheer walls of the two fjords, the small villages and farms tucked into every available shelf of land and the lacy ribbons of water flowing over the cliffs combine to say to you, "This is Norway at its Best."

Gudvangen is a small village located at the top end of Nærøyfjord. It is essentially a residential village, but where car ferries dock, there is a nice visitor's center with a gift shop. And there are a few small hotels that cater to those who are traveling through the fjord country either by car, utilizing the combination of roads and ferryboat connections or the more physically active who are hiking, walking or cycling their way around the country. The earliest hotel to open in Gudvangen was in 1830. Gudvangen is also connected directly to Fläm by way of the Gudvangen Tunnel that cuts through the mountain separating the two fjords. However, the dock is not large enough to accommodate any size cruise ship, thus it becomes necessary to anchor off shore and tender guests to the dock. Once in Gudvangen there is not much to do other than walk around the town and enjoy both its traditional wood architecture and the towering cliffs that surround it. The village is literally surrounded by waterfalls, a sight that is sure to please any camera enthusiast.

Gudvangen dates back to Viking times, and it has been a gathering place and small market center for approximately 1,000 years. Today there is a Viking festival held each year in late July or early August on the meadow located across the small river just east of the town. Locals dressed in traditional garb camp here in Viking fashion, performing traditional tasks, playing musical instruments and preparing food in the manner of their distant ancestors. There is a small admission fee, but this also entitles you to photograph the participants at your leisure.

MEMORIES: Every time I have visited both Fläm and Gudvangen I have found it to be a day filled with incredible, but ever changing scenery. The mood of the landscape will depend upon the weather, but even in the worst case scenario where it rains, there is still an aura of environmental magic to the entire length of Sognefjord

A detailed map of Aurlandsfjorden and Nærøyfjord (© OpenStreetMap contributors)

Sailing into Sognafjord en route to Aurlandsfjorden

Aurlandsfjorden on a dramatic misty morning

The small village of Undredal on Aurlandsfjorden

The village of Fläm seen from on board ship

The colorful houses of Fläm

Boarding the Flämsbana train for the trip to Myrdal

Traveling on the Flämsbana, passing small villages

Climbing high into the mountains on the Flämsbana

There are so many waterfalls along the Flämsbana to dazzle the eye

The Flämsbana highlight is stopping at the base of this thundering waterfall

Sailing up Nærøyfjord to Gudvangen

Nærøyfjord is very majestic in late afternoon light

Traditional Gudvangen architecture

There is a quiet charm to the village of Gudvangen

In late summer the Viking festival is one of the Gudvangen highlights

NORDFJORDEN
VISITING OLDEN

The Nordfjorden system and the location of Olden (© OpenStreetMap contributors)

Visting Olden after having sailed through the Sognefjord system the prior day if your are sailing northbound, stopping at Fläm and Gudvangen, is almost reaching for sensory overload. Just when you thought you had seen some of the most beautiful scenery Norway has to offer, the next day you are waking up to a majestic landscape that rivals what you had just seen. If your itinerary is one in which you visit the Norfjorden system first and then sail on the following day to Fläm and Gudvangen, the same condition will apply. Which fjord system is more majestic? The answer to that question is purely subjective and a matter of taste. As one who has made the journey many times, I cannot give a definitive answer. Although I must say that the village of Olden and the chain of lakes south to the head of the Jostedalsbreen Ice Sheet is one of the most stunning landscapes in the country. And if you happen to visit on a day with dappled light, that is a mix of sun and cloud, you will experience the true magic of Norway.

Norfjorden is among the longer fjord systems in Norway, its total length being just over 106 kilometers or 63 miles. In its upper reaches, since most of its runoff comes from the large Jostedalsbreen Ice Sheet, which some maps refer to as a glacier, through four small tributary fjords that come together to form the primary Norfjord. Jostedalsbreen is the largest single mass of ancient glacial ice on the European continent, exceeded in size only by the large ice sheets of Iceland, which is a European country culturally, but not a part of mainland Europe geologically. The village of Olden is located where the rushing waters of the Oldelva River flows into Faleidfjorden, a small extension of the larger Norfjorden, it being one arm of Norfjord. The glacial melt comes from the Birksdalsbreen Glacier, which is an arm of the larger Jostedalsbreen Ice Sheet. It is located around 40 kilometers or 24 miles south of Olden, at the top end of the valley carved initially by the glacier thousands of years ago, and today fed by the Oldeelva River.

Because of the depth of glacial scour, these fjords are especially deep, here where Faleidfjorden flows into Norfjorden it is 565 meters or 1,854 feet deep. There is no ship in the world that would have any difficulty navigating in water this deep, however, the largest cruise ships cannot be accommodated with docking facilities and the town of Olden cannot handle thousands of ship guests at one time. So the limiting factor in whether your itinerary includes a stop in Olden is not determined by the act of navigation, but rather by the inability of small villages to service the needs of large numbers of visitors at the same time. Thus if you truly want to enjoy cruising through most of the fjords of Norway, you are best off in choosing a ship that carries 500 passengers or less.

VISITING OLDEN: It takes around four hours to sail all the way through Norfjorden to the village of Olden. There is a single dock, and given that this is not a major cruise destination, it is doubtful that more than one cruise ship will be in port at a given time. Being able to dock does make the visit easier, as you do not need to spend time waiting for and then riding the tender boat to or from shore.

The Olden area is surprisingly old with regard to settlement. Evidence shows that pre Viking settlement can be traced back to the Iron Age. But the actual village of Olden is relatively young by Norwegian standards with settlement dating back to the mid 1600's, but there were scattered households at the top end of the fjord as far back as the early 1300's. The old church located in the heart of the village was built in 1759, but on the same site there was once an old stave church built back in the 1300's.

Within the Olden region, back in 1905 and again in 1936, there was a massive avalanche of rock that toppled off of Mt. Ramnefjelt into Lovatnet Lake, creating a massive series of tsunami waves that killed 102 people in the two disasters combined. This to date is the largest loss of life from any natural catastrophe in the history of Norway. Some cruise operators do offer a hike to Lovatnet Lake, not with the past disaster in mind, but for guests to simply enjoy the breathtaking scenery.

Although the village only has a resident population of 500, it is becoming more oriented to the cruise industry. There are a few local tour operators and a hop on hop off bus that meet the ship and offer affordable tours through the town and to the front of the Birksdalsbreen Glacier. And most cruise lines also offer one or more scenic tours. Apart from some cruise lines having a hike to Lovatnet Lake, most offer a coach tour to visit the Birksdalsbreen Glacier. These tours do involve a bit of hiking in order to reach viewpoints that are advantageous in seeing the glacier. And some cruise operators offer a longer coach tour to visit the more massive Jostedalsbreen Ice Sheet. Visiting Olden is all about the natural landscape, as the village itself offers only the old church and its lovely houses, sights that can be enjoyed in a matter of minutes.

DINING OUT: Olden is such a small village, and choice is very limited. Lunch is possible if you do not go on a group tour, but the majority of guests generally return to the ship given the meager selection of restaurants.
* Molla Gjesthus - Located opposite where the ship docks, is a small guesthouse with limited offerings of food and drink. It is very expensive, but it does provide local color and has a friendly staff.
* Yris Kafe - Located in the heart of Olden, and often showing up in guide books as Per's Cafe, this small establishment offers light lunches and the prices are reasonable by Norwegian standards.

Sailing up Norfjorden at dawn

Along the shoreline of Norfjorden in the early morning hours

Sailing into Olden

First view of Olden from the ship

The beauty of the top end of the fjord at Olden

The interior of the old 17th century church in Olden

The fast flowing Oldelva River

The beauty of Oldelva Lake

The magnificent beauty of Upper Lake nearest the glacier

Dozens of small streams run into both Oldelva and Upper Lakes

The face of the Birksdalsbreen Glacier

ÅLESUND

A map of the region of Ålesund (© OpenStreetMap contributors)

A visit to Ålesund comes as quite a surprise to those who are simply expecting another Norwegian town or village. Ålesund is a significant coastal city with a metro area population of approximately 49,000 residents. Both the physical setting and the architecture of the city make it quite distinctive and to some degree unique among the coastal ports of Norway.

THE PHYSICAL LANDSCAPE: Ålesund is a city of islands. It is located at a junction of several fjords that came together during the last glacial advance, carving up the landscape in such a way that when the ice melted back and sea level rose, numerous offshore islands were created. Ålesund is connected by one of the channels between the islands to the entrance of Geirangerfjorden, the most visited of all of the fjords of Norway. The city actually occupies portions of seven different islands. The surrounding islands, including those that are a part of Ålesund are rocky, but not very prominent. And as is true in most of Norway below the Arctic Circle they are thickly covered in coniferous forest or woodland. The higher mountains from which the fjords originate are visible from Ålesund and their snow-covered peaks add to the overall beauty of the landscape.

The waters surrounding Ålesund are calm most of the time, but can become quite choppy when the wind picks up at any time of year. Once beyond the islands, the waters of the North Sea can be quite stormy, especially in winter and often during short summer gales.

The region still falls within the maritime climate regime similar to that of Bergen and the other ports to the south. But being that the high mountains are a bit farther to the east, the rainfall totals are slightly lower and there are a few more sunny days than in Bergen, Haugesund or Stavanger.

A BRIEF HISTORY: Viking legend dates back to a famous warrior in the 10th century named Rollo who came from a village just northwest of present day Ålesund, showing that the area has an long history.

But the city of Ålesund itself only dates back to the early 19th century, being founded as a town in 1838. The city center of today, however, owes its unique existence to a great fire that occurred in 1904, destroying most of town because of very strong winds that fanned the flames into a conflagration. Prior to the great fire, Kaiser Wilhelm of Germany used to vacation here and when he heard about this terrible fire, he sent both building supplies to build shelters that would temporarily house the community. The actual rebuilding was done after initial shelter was provided, and it was decided to utilize the Art Nouveau style, which was so popular, especially in Germany. Architects and builders trained in the style were brought in to help in the rebuilding, making Ålesund a classic example today of Art Nouveau. It is so well recognized and it has an interpretative center and it is active in the Europe wide network to preserve this as an important architectural style.

What fed the Ålesund economy until the mid 1930's, was fishing, in particular for herring. But the local fishermen ultimately destroyed their bounty by devising better ways to catch the fish. By the mid 1930's, the stock became so depleted that the industry died. Today there is limited fishing, but it no longer is the mainstay of the Ålesund economy. The city has become an important regional trade center, and that is now its primary role.

During World War II Ålesund was a major hot bed for resistance, much of with close ties to the British who aided in getting many people out of the country despite the Nazi occupation. The invading military did not use

Ålesund for any major activities and most allied raids were on installations farther to the north, thus sparing much damage to the architecture or infrastructure.

After the war, as Ålesund began to assume more of a regional role, new business and bank buildings in the city center led initially to the destruction of numerous of the old Art Nouveau buildings. And although they were the pride of the city, there was little to no attempt to spare them. There were even those in the community that openly welcomed the new developments as a sign that Ålesund was modernizing. One development that did bring total approval was the linking of the various islands within the city and beyond, bringing a more cohesive transportation pattern into being.

By the 1970's, as more demolition took place to bring in further development a backlash developed and there were demonstrations against the ongoing destruction of the city's unique architectural heritage. As a result, today Ålesund is very protective of its post 1904 fire revival, and Art Nouveau is very much a selling point in the community. The city has continued to grow and the modern development is now seen east of the city center in areas that have grown out of the former woodland and farms, and this has been welcomed, but no longer at the expense of the city center. And today there is an amazing network of tunnels and bridges interconnecting Ålesund with its surroundings, thus making it even more the market and business center that it has become.

More cruise ships now visit Ålesund, and fortunately the main docks are right in the very heart of the city. Thus it is very easy for walking tours to be conducted or for visitors to go off on their own and explore the city center.

VISITING ÅLESUND: Depending upon your cruise line, there may be several tours offered to either some of the outlying islands or to the mountainous interior, as each cruise line has its own agenda as to what they choose to provide. This section of the chapter will, however, be confined to Ålesund, showing you the major sights that are capable of being seen within the local area.

*   Fjellstua Overlook is the number one visitor attraction in Ålesund, especially during clear weather. Rising up just east of the city center is the mountain known as Aksla where the Fjellstua Lodge is perched with its outdoor deck providing a dramatic view over the city and well out to sea or eastward into the fjords. You can reach the top on your own, if you have the strength to negotiate 418 steps that will climb the side of the mountain. Or you can hire a taxi to take you to the top, wait for the short time you will spend

viewing the panorama and then return you to the city center. But all of the city tours that the various cruise lines offer do include a drive to the top of Aksla to enjoy the view.

* Atlantic Sea Park is usually the second most popular attraction, but it is not located in the city center. It is at the western end of the city via a bridge that connects central Ålesund with Hessa. It is walkable, about five kilometers or three miles, but again it is easiest to take a taxi. Again most of the tours will include a stop at the Atlantic Sea Park. The focus is the aquarium that highlights the sea life of this region, and their outdoor exhibits do include penguins even though they are from the Southern Hemisphere and were never found in Norway. The park does put on a show with their seals, which both adults and children find very endearing. The park is open from 11 AM to 4 PM daily, and remains open to 6 PM on Sunday.

* Jugendstilsenteret and Kunstmuseet Kube is the most important museum to visit to learn about Ålesund after the 1904 fire and the development of Art Nouveau. It is just steps from where the ships dock, located at Apotekergata # 16. It is open from 11 AM to 4 PM on days when the ship is in port. This is in effect two museums for the price of one admission. A visit gives you the story of the city of Ålesund and of the Art Nouveau movement. And there is a small, but interesting museum shop. A visit then makes the architecture of the city center far more meaningful.

* Ålesunds Museum is also in the city center, located at Rasmus Rosennebergs gate #16 and open daily between 11 AM and 3 PM daily, but closed on weekends. Allow at least an hour or more. The museum is devoted to the history of Ålesund and also to the importance of the fishing industry in the city's growth.

* Waldenhuset Museum enables you to have a look at how Ålesund looked before the great fire, as it is the only house to survive, now a museum depicting local life. It is a short walk from the city center, located at Grensegata #6 and open when ships are in port. There is also an interesting story of divine help that saved the house, but I will not spoil it by telling you any more. The ladies who run the museum will offer you coffee and delicious homemade cake as part of your visit.

* Sunnmoere Museum is located a short distance east of the city and you will need to have a taxi or be on a tour to visit, but it is well worth the effort. During summer, the museum is open daily from 10 AM to 4 PM and Saturday from Noon to 4 PM with Sunday hours being from 10 AM to 4 PM. This is essentially a spacious outdoor museum that recreates Norwegian life through a number of houses and buildings along with having a display of Viking relics. The setting is very conducive to strolling about and each building presents a glimpse of life as it was. Many visitors consider this to be the best sightseeing venue in Ålesund.

*   Alnes Lighthouse is a very popular attraction. It is located on the outer island of Godøy, which is reached by way of a series of bridges and tunnels, showing you the way in which these settled islands are all linked to Ålesund. The ride there and back is worth the visit alone. You will need to be on a tour, providing one is offered, or you can negotiate a rate with a local taxi for the drive there and back. The modern lighthouse dates only to 1936, and its architectural style is unique in that it built with four flat, angular walls capping out at 225 meters or 738 feet in height. The lighthouse also has a small museum to help you understand its role, and it is still active in its function as a beacon for mariners. There is a cultural center adjacent to the lighthouse and a small cafe that provides refreshments and light meals.
*   Giske Kirke is a small regional church on the island of Giske, which is en route to the Alnes Lighthouse. The church dates to the 11th century and is well preserved, giving you a glimpse into early Christian life in Viking Norway.

This is not an exhaustive list, but presents you with the most important sights in Ålesund. But during your one day stop you must allow a couple of hours simply to wander the streets of the old inner city and soak up the architectural flavor. If your cruise does stay overnight, and if the weather is favorable, the city takes on a very beautiful glow when the sun is low in the western sky. During summer there is only a brief hour or two of darkness, but Ålesund looks so especially rich during the golden hours of late evening sun.

DINING OUT: Unless your ship should just happen to stay overnight, which is rather rare on fjord itineraries, you will be able to at least have lunch in Ålesund. Here are my recommendations for traditional Norwegian restaurants in Ålesund.

*   Cafe Lyspunktet located in the city center on Kipervikgata #1 is ideal for lunch. It opens at Noon and stays open until 9 PM. They have a good menu selection including soups, sandwiches and fresh seafood dishes. Their fish soup is exceptionally good. It can become crowded at lunch, and reservations are not taken.
*   Anno is located in the center of town at Apotekergata #9 and open from early morning to mid evening, serving all three meals. For lunch they can get rather busy, but if you come in after 1 PM, it is quiet and the service is very friendly. They are known for their fresh seafood and also pizza, but with a Norwegian twist in that you can have a salmon pizza. The combination of good, fresh food and fast service enables you to still have plenty of time for sightseeing.
*   Brasserie Normandie is a relatively expensive, but high quality restaurant in the Hotel Parc Scandic located at Storgata #16. It opens at Noon and remains

open until 11 PM. Their menu is diverse, but with a strong emphasis upon fresh seafood, and good desserts. Service is not rushed, sometimes even a bit slow. But the atmosphere is relaxed.

* Lyst is a very nice, traditional restaurant located in the city center on Kongens gate #12 and open from 10 to 1 AM. Again I recommend going later for lunch, as they do get rather busy. They offer a good selection of traditional and contemporary dishes with an emphasis on freshness, especially the seafood.

SHOPPING: There are several small souvenir stores, and also a few stores selling maritime antiques all located in the city center. But Ålesund is not a destination for any real high quality arts and crafts shopping. For that I do recommend the larger cities such as Bergen, Trondheim and Tromsø.

The city center of Ålesund (© OpenStreetMap contributors)

Sailing into the harbor at Ålesund

The city center of Ålesund with Aksla above it

The more modern housing of Ålesund on the slopes of Aksla

A close up of Ålesund housing on the slopes of Aksla

Ålesund from the top of Aksla

Close up of the far western side of Ålesund from Aksla

A view out to the island of Giska from Aksla

A Midsummer Eve bonfire tower on the shores of Ålesund

Along the Ålesundet running through the heart of the city

Examples of Art Nouveau style along the Ålesundet

The heart of the city close up from Aksla

The city's main pedestrian shopping street

Maritime antiques in a downtown store window

The Waldenhuset Museum - The house surviving the 1904 fire

The Sunnmøere Museum (Work of Andrava, CC BY SA 3.0, Wikimedia.org)

The Alnes Lighthouse (Work of Concierge.2C, CC BY SA 3.0, Wikimedia.org)

STORFJORDEN
VISITING HELLESYLT & GEIRANGER

Storfjorden (© OpenStreetMap contributors)

Every visitor to Norway comes away with his or her favorite fjord. In reality it is difficult to say which is the more beautiful, as each has its own level of majesty and its own level of spectacular scenery. But there is a very strong favoritism shown to the Storfjorden system with its two beautiful tributary fjords of Sunnylvsfjorden (Hellesylt) and Geirangerfjorden. Many of the fjords see few if any cruise ships, but both the small ports of Hellesylt and Geiranger are especially popular destinations, and they appear on Norwegian calendars and travel posters quite regularly. It is difficult to say why these two have become the so called "poster children" for cruising the fjords of Norway other than the fact that they are the most spectacular of the southern fjord region that is reached easily on a seven-day cruise from Copenhagen or Oslo. I strongly believe this popularity developed out of proximity, as other fjords of

equal or even greater magnificence lie much farther to the north of Storfjorden and thus require a longer cruise.

SAILING INTO STORFJORDEN: The distance to Hellesylt and Geiranger from the open sea requires several hours of sailing. Most cruise itineraries have the ship entering Storfjorden at around 6 AM in order to reach Hellesylt by 10 AM and Geiranger at around Noon or slightly earlier. I know most people like to sleep in during the early morning hours, especially if they attended a show or visited the casino the night before. But in doing so, you will miss some exceptionally spectacular scenery, especially if the weather is good. And in Norway that is always the big "if" factor.

Storfjorden initially begins with lower mountains closest to the sea and the shorelines are gentle with small villages and numerous farms. As your ship proceeds inward, the mountains progressively close in, at times framing the fjord with steep cliffs that are so close that the telltale scratches created by glacial scour are visible. Waterfalls are so numerous where streams plunge down into the fjord. Once the small streams that are now high above would have merged gently with the former river system now flooded by the sea after the glaciers scoured the valleys to such great depths. These waterfalls are referred to as "hanging valleys." And even if you are not particularly interested in their geologic origin, you will be mesmerized by their intense beauty.

HELLESYLT: By mid morning, your ship may turn into Sunnylvsfjorden, which is a short channel that ends at the tiny village of Hellesylt. Not all cruise ships will stop here, as there are no dock facilities and the village is too tiny to host large numbers of visitors. Only those cruise ships with itineraries that offer an all day bus tour through the mountains to rejoin the ship at Geiranger will stop and tender those guests on shore to meet their coach. For those remaining on board, with binoculars you can take a visit to this tiny village and see its thundering whitewater river that empties into Sunnylvsfjorden.

GEIRANGERFJORDEN: Most ships will proceed to enter Geirangerfjorden directly from Storfjorden, with the day's destination being the resort village of Geiranger. It will take up to 90 minutes for your ship to sail the length of Geirangerfjorden, passing between towering cliffs where numerous waterfalls are plunging into the deep waters of the fjord.

The most noted feature you will see on the port (left) side of the ship while sailing in will be the Seven Sisters Waterfall. This hanging valley feature results from a sizable river atop the cliffs that is clogged with numerous large boulders that clog the channel thus forcing the water to distribute itself into seven distinct channels before plunging down the face of the cliff, dropping a length of 410 meters or 1,350 feet. It is at its most spectacular flow in late spring and early summer, fed by the melting snow in the higher country above. The water splashes and dashes down the cliff face and when the sun is shining directly above, a beautiful rainbow is created. According to Norse legend, these falls represent seven playful maidens who are flirting with the giant single waterfall across the fjord known as the Suitor. He is also attempting to win their attention, but the primary Norse God is keeping him apart by the depth of the fjord.

GEIRANGER: After passing the Seven Sisters, the ship will round a bend in the fjord and there before you is the village of Geiranger clinging to the shore line. The town with only 300 full time residents is filled with numerous guest houses, hotels and restaurants, as it is a major gathering place for visitors who are exploring the interior glaciers, lakes and meadows. Geiranger is one of Norway's major tourist destinations. And then entire fjord and surrounding mountain region has been given UNESCO World Heritage Site status.

There is only one small dock in Geiranger and thus most cruise ships will anchor in the fjord and tender guests on shore during their stay. But fortunately the waters are always calm and the distance from the ship to the shore is less than one kilometer. Once on shore, you will either join a motor coach for one of several tours into the high glacial valleys to both enjoy the scenery and the views down upon Geirangerfjorden. Or if you are not comfortable with winding roads and great heights, it is best to simply wander about Geiranger and enjoy the views from lower perspectives.

One of the most exciting and beautiful sights in Geiranger is the cascading river that rushes down from the high glacier to the fjord. There is a massive stairway you can follow from the top end of the fjord that will take you along this thundering torrent all the way up to the high part of Geiranger where you can then follow the main Route 63 back into town, past the Grande Hotel. It is the highlight of walking around in Geiranger.

While on shore, you can dine and sample local Norwegian cuisine. I recommend lunch at the following:
* Brasserie Posten - Located along the Stranda or waterfront, this restaurant is highly rated for its fish soups, fish cakes and fresh vegetables and salads. And of course no Norwegian meal is complete without delicate desserts. But keep in mind that this is a tourist destination and good food is expensive. The restaurant opens at 10:30 AM and remains open until 10 PM.

* Grande Fjord Hotel - Located high above the waterfront on the main road, Route 53. It is one of the larger hotels and impossible to miss. They serve lunch from Noon onward. Their menu is extensive and of course fish soups, fresh fish, fish cakes and salads are very much a part of what is offered. There are also meat dishes for those wanting to indulge in a heavier meal. And adding to the delicious food is a spectacular view from their picture windows.

* Westeras Gard - Located high above Geiranger on a rather steep walking path that is not recommended for those unable to follow a steep grade. But if you are able to negotiate the path, the view is spectacular. And the food is also excellent, again serving a varied menu. However, roasted goat is considered to be a house specialty. For dessert, they do serve traditional waffles with ice cream and a rich sauce.

* Cafe Ole - In the heart of Geiranger's main shopping area and open from 9 AM to 5 PM. I would recommend this cafe for light fare, especially desserts and hot chocolate or excellent coffee.

SAILING OUT: If you still have not had enough scenery for one day, you might want to spend time out on deck or in your ship's forward observation lounge during the long sail out through Sognefjorden back to sea. From the time you leave Geiranger it will take about five hours to reach the open sea. And as the day progresses and the sun dips lower on the western horizon, the mountains and shoreline take on a very special glow. It is almost impossible to put into words the majestic aura that is created in the evening light. And few shipboard guests take the chance to enjoy the vistas. I have watched the entire sail out from Geiranger, even missing dinner, just to be able to absorb the changing moods. And clearly I will enjoy it again in 2017 on two sailings out from Geiranger. It is easy to understand why this is such a popular destination. It is especially beautiful, filled with majestic views and it is in closer proximity to Copenhagen or Oslo to be accessible on shorter cruises than fjords much farther to the north.

Entering Storfjorden in the early morning

The village of Hellesylt and its thundering river

Entering Geirangerfjorden

The Seven Sisters Waterfall in Geirangerfjorden

A closer view of the Seven Sisters Waterfall

Arriving at Geiranger

Following the Geiranger River with its whitewater rapids

The beauty of the Geiranger River

At the top of the Geiranger River's stairway

High above Geiranger on the way to the glaciers

Up in the glacial ice fields high above Geiranger

A dramatic view from high above Geirangerfjorden

Storfjorden in the early evening while sailing out toward the sea

Approaching the sea from Storfjorden at 11 PM

KRISTIANSUND

The coastal islands around Kristiansund (© OpenStreetMap contributors)

Kristiansund is the major city and administrative center in the Nordmøe region just north of Storfjorden. Not all cruise ships make a stop at this city whose history celebrates the one time importance of cod fishing. Today Kristiansund is very much a blue collar city that supports various maintenance projects out on the North Sea oil drilling platforms. With a population of around 20,000, it is a substantial community, but one that many cruise passengers do not find as enjoyable because most of its historic architecture perished during World War II.

THE GEOGRAPHIC SETTING: Kristiansund is a city by the sea, yet it turns its back to the harsh North Sea and faces inward, clustered on four islands around a sheltered central harbor. The city is quite densely populated, as its 20,000 residents occupy only 7.9 square kilometers, thus making it one of the country's most concentrated cities. Yet you will not feel a sense of crowding because of the fact that the city climbs steep hillsides on all four of its islands and the high ground is topped off by beautiful woodland. Facing out to sea on the back side of the northern and western island, the land shows its rugged granite base, offering no beaches or safe anchorage. And in winter, it can be lashed by strong wind and surf.

Despite its island location, its proximity to the mainland has enabled Kristiansund to be connected by bridges and thus it does not quite feel like it is isolated from the rest of the nation. And it is also connected to a string of islands on which there are small fishing villages by a series of under sea tunnels and bridges known as the Great Atlantic Road. Apart from its very scenic potential and it being an architectural wonder, it is part of a very extensive system of roads that connect many of the near offshore islands to the mainland all along the Norwegian coast. The country has invested heavily in its infrastructure.

Kristiansund's climate is that of a temperate marine regime. Summers are relatively cool and sunny days are interspersed with cloudy periods that bring rain showers. When visiting in the summer, it is rather hit or miss as to having a bright sunny day.

Being closer to the Arctic Circle, Kristiansund has long winter nights with very short days, but its snowfall accumulation is far less than cities that are sheltered from the sea by way of being on the inner channels or deep into the fjords. But temperatures are still cold, hovering around the freezing mark.

THE FASCINATING HISTORY: To appreciate your visit to Kristiansund it is important to have some understanding of the city's history. The first thing that will strike you when sailing into the harbor is the lack of a sense of history in its architecture. And this is part of the overall story of the city.

The Norwegian coast has a long history of settlement. There is archaeological evidence of pre Viking tribes having moved north along the edges of the retreating glacial ice as far back as 10,000 years ago. With the melt water mixing with sea water, high nutrient plankton provided a base for a rich and diverse marine population of shellfish and fish, and this encouraged human settlement along the coast.

Although during Viking times there were various battles fought in the immediate area, Kristiansund was never known to have been settled by the Norse warrior tribes.

During the Middle Ages, as Christianity was extending into Norway and the Norse tribes were settling down and developing more of a sedentary life, only the small island of Grip, off the coast from Kristiansund, saw any development as a fishing port. And it is assumed that the fishermen would have exploited the waters around what is now Kristiansund. An early Christian stave church is believed to have been built in 1470 in the village of Grip. The island continues to be inhabited to the present day, and it is connected during the summer by ferry to Kristiansund, a journey of approximately 30-minutes. But Grip does face the full fury of North Sea storms and the island has been swamped many times.

Kristiansund only dates to the mid 1600's, when the first fishermen began to settle here. By the late 1600's, there was sufficient settlement based upon fishing and lumber to warrant the establishment of a government customs outpost. But it was in the waning years of the 17th century that Kristiansund's future was determined. Thanks to the introduction of the technique for drying cod, then a plentiful and bountiful species, was introduced. And with a ready market in countries such as Portugal and Spain, Kristiansund became one of the most important fishing ports along the Norwegian coast. Known in the Norwegian language as "klippfisk," salted and dried cod was a basic staple to feed the hungry populations of the Iberian Peninsula and other parts of the western Mediterranean.

The importance of klippfisk is what put Kristiansund on the map, the town being given a city charter in 1742. The growth of Kristiansund was facilitated by the abundance of timber, and apart from the main church and the 19th century concert hall, the majority of buildings consisted of wood siding. There were occasional outbreaks of fire, but it was not until World War II and the Nazi occupation of Norway that Kristiansund would see a major conflagration. To exhort submission prior to occupying the port for military purposes, the German air force firebombed Kristiansund, destroying most of the community. Only the stone buildings survived to the present day. This is why Kristiansund lacks a distinctive architecture, as the majority of the city is of post World War II origin.

One of the most tragic moments of the Nazi occupation of the city was the rounding up of 18 Jewish citizens that ranged in age from five up into the 70's. They were shipped off to one of the concentration/death camps and nobody survived to return to Kristiansund. There is a small memorial in the park just up the hill from the city center and opposite the modern city church.

With the discovery of oil in the North Sea, Kristiansund became one of the major service centers for the oil drilling and pumping platforms just over the horizon out at sea. The city also is home to the families of many of the oil workers who commute between the city and the platforms, living out at sea for periods of time before returning to the city. This has brought new life to Kristiansund since cod fishing has been greatly diminished by the declining numbers of fish and strict quotas as to their harvesting.

Tourism plays a small role in the city's economy because it is not located in one of the most scenic of areas, and it is not easy to reach in contrast to the many fjords where there is a strong tourist focus. Few cruise ships call in at Kristiansund, but for those that do, the people are quite welcoming.

WHAT TO SEE AND DO: Much will depend upon your cruise line with regard to tours outside of Kristiansund. Some of the smaller more upmarket cruise lines offer a tour by motor coach along the Great Ocean Road, which can be quite spectacular on a nice sunny day. Some cruise lines offer more adventure oriented kayaking or sailing tours, and on occasion I have seen a tour to the historic island of Grip.

The most commonly offered tour is a four-hour guided tour by motor coach around the city of Kristiansund with a visit to the klippfisk museum where you learn the history of cod fishing, salting and drying and its impact upon the growth of the city. But many will choose to simply walk the community, and if that is your choice, here are the major highlights:

* Sundbaten - This yellow ferry boat that you will see at the World War II monument with the surrounding Norwegian flags is one quick way to spend time visiting all of the islands that make up the city. It travels in a counterclockwise direction, so you can either stay on for the entire ride or get off and catch some of the recommended sights. The ferry runs quite often and has its schedule posted.

* Kirkelandet Kirke - This ultra modern new church has replaced the old stone church across the harbor as the main Lutheran church for the city. It has beautiful stained glass windows and is worth a short visit.

* Holocaust Memorial - Just down the hill from the church about one full block in the park is the memorial, which is somewhat hidden away. It is a very poignant reminder of the Holocaust and its impact upon Kristiansund.

* Varden Tower - This is the best way to get a visual overview of the city. It is a short distance from the city center, but it is not well marked. Stop at the local tourist office in the city center to ask specific directions. Essentially you start at the new church on the hill above the city center, follow the main street, which is Langveien for one long block to Vuggaveien and turn left, the right at the first cross street, which is Hagbart Brinchmanns vei and you will see the path to the tower on your left. The tower has a button at the door and when pressed, it triggers an automatic opener.

* Mellemvaerftet Shipbuilding Museum - Located down a steep hill from the main strand that runs along the harbor. This rather small museum is really for those who have a special interest in how the old fishing vessels were built back in the time period when Kristiansund was at the height of its cod fishing period. It is open all day, especially when a cruise ship is in port.
* Bautean - This is the high hill where the canon is fired to welcome a cruise ship into port. It is a bit of a climb, but well worth the imposing view of the city and out to the surrounding islands. You can reach it by walking across the high bridge to Innlandet Island or by taking the ferry boat and getting off at the first stop.
* Norwegian Klippfisk Museum - This is a major feature on the ship sponsored tour, but if you want to go on your own, you will need to take a taxi as it is too far to walk. You can take the ferryboat, getting off at the final stop, but it is a steep walk up to the museum. The guided tour is quite fascinating and it surprises you how much there is to learn.
* Nordlandet Kirke - On the Nordlandet Island, which is the second ferry stop, you can see this old stone church up close. It is built of stone, but only dates back to 1914, and is one of the few buildings to survive the bombing of World War II.

DINING OUT: Kristiansund has numerous restaurants, but you must remember that this is a blue collar community of fishermen and oil workers So do not expect gourmet quality or ambiance. I have eaten lunch in Kristiansund numerous times over the years, and these are my recommendations:
* Sjostjerna - Located in the city center on Skolegata. It is open from Noon to 11 PM and serves genuine Norwegian cuisine, primarily specializing in fresh fish and seafood. Bot the food and service are good, and the atmosphere is typical of the cozy restaurants of the city. One of the specialties is bacalao, which is the Portuguese way of reconstituting dried and salted cod. It is very good and now accepted as a local delicacy. If fiskeboller are on the menu, it is my favorite. It is made from chopped fish that is formed into what would be like meatballs and then poached in a fish broth.
* Bryggekanten Brasserie - Located along the waterfront near to where cruise ships dock. It has a good reputation for quality cuisine and service. And it has great views of the harbor. Open from 11:30 AM to 10:30 PM, you will not go wrong dining here. They offer a variety of seafood and meat dishes, including burgers to satisfy those from North America.
* Nordmorskafeen Homemade Food - Located along the waterfront at Fosnagata #3 upstairs, and open from 9 AM to 6 PM, this is my favorite place for traditional, well-prepared Norwegian dishes. It is not fancy, and you order at the counter and then select your beverage and dessert. When the main course is ready, it is brought to your table. The staff is very friendly and will

make substitutions to accommodate your tastes. Their menu is small, but changes daily. I have never had a bad lunch here.

If you are simply in the mood for dessert, the shopping mall across the street from where the ship docks has a very good pastry counter on the second floor. They offer sandwiches and pastries with coffee or tea, and it can sometimes be just the light snack you are looking for.

The four islands of Kristiansund (© OpenStreetMap contributors)

The main city of Kristiansund (© OpenStreetMap contributors)

The outer suburbs of Kristiansund on Innlandet Island

Docking in the town center of Kristiansund

The firing of the welcoming canon from Innlandet Island summit

The main waterfront strand seen from onboard ship

One of the oil platform service vessels docked in the city center

On the waterfront in the city center with its war monument

Much of downtown Kristiansund is quite hilly so when out walking you will get plenty of exercise

There are beautiful flower plantings all through the city center of Kristiansund

The war memorial to the 18 Kristiansund Jews who were sent off to the Nazi death camps during World War II

The inscriptions on the Kristiansund Holocaust Memorial showing the names and ages of the victims

Summer is strawberry season in Kristiansund

Fresh cut flowers for sale in the Kristiansund Mall

Typical post World War II house construction in Kristiansund

TRONDHEIMSFJORDEN
VISITING TRONDHEIM

The surroundings of Trondheim (© OpenStreetMap contributors)

Trondheim is one of four major cities in Norway, and it is the farthest north of the large cities. Oslo and Bergen are the number one and two cities with regard to size, but then there is a brewing argument between Stavanger and Trondheim as to which city is the third largest. Even at the time of writing this book, there is no agreement among various Norwegian or foreign sources as to giving a definitive answer. Essentially it is a matter of whether suburban areas are included and if so, how far out from the city center the source counts communities as suburbs. In 2016 when I was last in Trondheim, everyone I spoke with was positive that their city is now Norway's third largest. The population of metropolitan Trondheim is around 200,000. Regardless of the ranking, Trondheim is one of the most beautiful cities in the country and also a very historic community.

GEOGRAPHIC SETTING: The city of Trondheim is located in the narrow valley of the Nidelva River at a point where the river empties into Trondheim Fjord. To the east and west of the city, the land rises abruptly into wooded hills that reach a maximum elevation of 565 meters or 1,854 feet. These hills provide a beautiful setting for the city, adding to its overall scenic quality.

Trondheim is the largest city in Norway at such far northerly latitude and is just shy of 24-hour daylight during several weeks of summer and then just shy of total darkness for the first few weeks of winter.

Being close to the sea, but just enough inland has an impact upon the overall climate of Trondheim. It is essential a modified maritime climate with very cold winters and mild summers. The gale force winds that can blow off the North Sea do not quite reach Trondheim. At the same time the very heavy snows of the interior do not occur in the city. Its winters show a mix of rain and snow and are not as severe as the latitude would give one to believe. Summer days are mild, interspersed with fog, cloud and sunshine.

THE CITY'S LONG HISTORY: Trondheim has a history extending back to the year 997, founded during the reign of King Olav Tryggvason, one of the first two great Viking leaders to accept Christianity. Trondheim, then known as Nidaros, became the archdiocese in 1152, under the Catholic faith and it also served as the secular capital of Norway until 1217 when it was moved to Oslo.

The great Romanesque and gothic cathedral of Nidaros still stands as the cornerstone of the city center of Trondheim. Its construction dates to 1070 when it was built to honor King Olaf II who was canonized and became the patron of Norway. But it suffered three fires during its long history and the present edifice dates to the early 18th century and is of course the seat of the Lutheran bishop and has been since the reformation.

As noted with reference to the cathedral experiencing several fires, this has been the fate of so many Norwegian cities in their early years because of the widespread use of wood for construction. Trondheim was no exception. The greatest fire occurred in 1651 when the major part of the city was destroyed. This did, however, lead to more careful rebuilding with the use of wider streets to prevent a block fire from easily spreading.

Norway and Sweden were drawn into the Danish dominated Kalmar Union in 1397, but Sweden withdrew in 1523, leaving Norway united with Denmark until 1814. However a brief war between Denmark and Sweden resulted in Trondheim briefly becoming Swedish territory from February 1658 until it was retaken less than a year later and validated by treaty in May 1660.

Norway was ceded to Sweden in 1814 through the Treaty of Kiel in which Denmark renounced all future claims. But in 1905, in an amicable arrangement Norway regained full independence. Trondheim never did, however, regain its political status, but the present king does enjoy frequent visits, staying it the small royal palace near the great cathedral.

The city of Trondheim was occupied by Nazi forces in early April 1940 and remained under harsh rule until the German surrender in May 1945. Given the deep fjord and its sheltered interior location, but with easy access to the sea, Trondheim became a major submarine base, remnants still visible to the present day. Citizens were under strict rules and regulations and penalties were harsh. However, the Norwegian resistance did inflict its share of retaliation all during the occupation. The German Navy had great plans to create a massive naval facility just outside of Trondheim, but fortunately they never realized their dream.

The modern history of Trondheim is still reflected in its old town district along the river where old wood warehouses, many now turned into fashionable lofts, recall the days when this was a major trade center. And overall there is a flavor of the city's Viking heritage seen in its architecture, and simply by the fact that such a major city exists this far north. And to reflect the city's early embrace of Christianity, the Nideros Cathedral stands as the most dominant downtown landmark. The city lays claim that it is the larges medieval building in all of Scandinavia, but I believe that the Lutheran cathedral in Uppsala, Sweden is every bit its equal in size.

SIGHTS TO SEE: There are few truly amazing sights to see in Trondheim, yet overall this is an interesting city because of the simple elegance of its old buildings and the stately character of the overall city. I believe that if you are on your own and hire a taxi, the best way to begin is with a broad overview. My suggestions are as follows:
* Viewpoint on the slopes of Steinberget - This viewpoint is just high enough to give you a sweeping panorama of the entire city and its surrounding hills. Yes there is an observation tower in the city that also contains a restaurant, but the viewpoint on Steinberget is quiet, out of the way, but close enough for a great first impression of Trondheim.
* Streets of the downtown and Olav Tryggvason Column - Next you should stop in the downtown and simply spend an hour walking the pleasant streets, taking in the mix of architectural styles and the overall ambiance. The massive column dedicated to the first Norwegian king to have made Trondheim his capital dominates the main downtown square.

* Niderosdomen - It is impossible to miss the imposing cathedral with its mix of gothic and Romanesque architectural styles. It is a massive structure sitting in a lush park and the most impressive building in the city.
* Old Town and Bridge - While in the city center, visit the preserved Old Town by walking across the beautiful bridge with its Viking carving, the original of which dated to 1681. The view from both the bridge and the far bank of the river is worth the effort.
* Kristiansten Fortress - Standing on a prominent hill southeast of the city center, this fortress offers a total panorama of the city from a perspective that is well within the urbanized area. It was built in 1681 after a devastating fire swept the main town. The purpose was to offer protection from any landward invasion coming via Sweden. It did see some action during the Great Northern War in 1718 when Swedish forces laid siege, but were unable to take the fortress. Although not a major facility, it is of great historic importance and also offers excellent views of the city.
* Ringve Museum - Located at Lade Alle #60 and open from 11 AM to 4 PM daily, this music housed in a rather large, old building is devoted to traditional music and the instruments used to play. This is a museum for those who are truly interested in the history of music, as there are few such museums in the world. And the surrounding gardens are also quite special.
* Rockheim Museum - Located on the waterfront at Brattoerkaia # 14 and open daily from 11 AM to 6 PM, this museum is devoted to popular Norwegian music. I only recommend it to those who are truly interested in contemporary music of the country you are visiting.
* Munkholmen - This island fortress combined monastery is very interesting because of its unique history. It is located in the fjord a short ferry ride from the downtown waterfront. Initially built by Benedictine monks in the 11th century, it became a prison/fortress in 1658. During World War II, Nazi forces occupied it to help protect their submarine base from Allied invasion.

DINING OUT: Depending upon your itinerary, you may or may not be in Trondheim during lunch. Many ships arrive in the early afternoon, leaving just before dinner, thus spending about five or six hours in the city. If your ship does spend the entire day, then it is worth taking the time to have a traditional Norwegian lunch. This is what I am recommending in those instances, and I have chosen four restaurants where such an experience can be had.
* Baklanded Skydsstation - Located at Ovre Bakklandet #33, and open from Noon to 1 AM, this is one of the most popular restaurants for a traditional Norwegian menu. The restaurant sits along the east side of the Nidelva River, facing the large park housing the cathedral. You will find that if you check any restaurant source, there are no bad reviews for this establishment. They

specialize in a variety of fresh fish and seafood dishes, and of course cod bacalao is one of the favorite entrees. And they also have traditional herring as an appetizer. If you are into sweet endings, there is a very rich hot chocolate along with a variety of Norwegian pastries.

* Ravnkloa Fish Market - Located along the waterfront at Monkegata #70 and open weekdays 10 AM to 5 PM and closing at 4 PM on weekends, this is a combination fish market and restaurant. They specialize in incredibly fresh fish and shellfish, cooked to perfection. You cannot get anything fresher given that the restaurant is on the docks where the fishing boats tie up. Two specialties are traditional creamy fish soup and fiskeboller - the cooked fish balls that are a major Norwegian delicacy.

Trondheim is a delightful city to visit because of its long history, exceptionally beautiful parks and architecture. And it is still a major center for fishing, thus having outstanding seafood restaurants.

Map of the city of Trondheim (© OpenStreetMap contributors)

Map of the city center of Trondheim (© OpenStreetMap contributors)

Looking at downtown Trondheim from Steinberget

Looking toward the cathedral in Trondheim from Steinberget

View over the walls of Kristiansten Fortress

Looking over the city from the Kristiansten Fortress

The Nideros Cathedral's Romanesque facade

Olav Tryggvason Gate in the city center

A mix of architectural styles on Brattørveita

Trondheim's official Royal Residence

Along the Nidelva River in the Old Town area

Typical wood houses of the mid 1900's overlooking the Nidelva River

The remaining houses of an 18th century fishing village

New high-rise apartments along the fjord west of the city center

THE LOFOTEN ISLANDS
VISITING SVOLVÆR

Map of the Lofoten Islands (© OpenStreetMap contributors)

The Lofoten Islands are a group of heavily glaciated islands that extend away from the Norwegian coast into the North Sea, creating an ever-narrowing gulf between themselves and the mainland known as Vestfjorden. But even these sheltered waters between the Lofoten Islands and the mainland can become quite choppy during even moderate weather. Thus if your cruise itinerary does include a stop in Svolvær or farther north in Harstadt, there is a very strong chance that you will not be able to land in Svolvær, but a more than 60 percent chance of docking in Harstadt. When I was last in this part of Norway during mid summer 2016, the morning of the ship's visit to Svolvær turned out to have a combination of low fog and moderate wind. The local pilots absolutely refused to grant entry into the port, so the ship had to sail on to Tromsø since Harstadt was not on the itinerary.

In spite of the difficulty often associated with landing in Svolvær, this is an especially striking part of Norway with regard to the beauty of its landscape.

The mountains rise quite abruptly from the sea, and there are numerous small bays and coves. The islands lie just north of the Arctic Circle, but given the proximity of the Gulf Stream, they have a more moderate climate than interior locations at their latitude. Water temperatures are kept above freezing throughout the winter, yet on the leeward sides of the islands, heavy snows can fall whereas on the windward side the snow level is far higher and rain predominates along the coast along with gale force winds. Summers are very mild and during spring there is actually a pronounced drier period with little to no rain and clear sunny days.

The island geography is very distinct, characterized by tall peaks that rise dramatically, the highest being 1,252 meters or 4,140 feet high. The lower slopes show a mix of lush grassland and wooded areas whereas the peaks are essentially barren. The nature of the rock layers, dating back to over 60,000,000 years, made them very susceptible to being eroded into their present form during the great ice age.

This is a region very rich in sea life, which has encouraged much fishing. On land there are many species of sea birds, otter and moose. Today only smaller minke whales frequent these islands because whaling is still practiced along the Norwegian coast, an economic activity controversial in the eyes of the world.

VISITING SVOLVÆR: If your ship visits the port of Svolvær you can consider yourself fortunate since this is a very picturesque small town set amid towering mountain peaks. There are several smaller fishing villages along the coast and depending upon what activities are planned by your cruise line, there may be small boat or land tours along the shoreline of the island of Austvågøya. It is a small town with only 4,500 permanent residents, yet its waterfront gives the illusion of this being a much larger community.

This area has a long history of settlement dating back to the early Viking era. The village of Vågar west of Svolvær can be dated back to approximately 800. Fishing and limited farming, especially the raising of dairy cattle have always been the main economic activities. Today with depleted cod stocks, many fishermen have turned to aquaculture, the farming of fish, especially of Atlantic salmon since there is a great market across Scandinavia for both fresh, smoked or cured salmon. The magnificent scenery combined with a series of bridges linking the islands and one major bridge connecting to the mainland, this has become an important vacation spot for Norwegian and other Scandinavian visitors. Foreign tourism apart from cruise passengers is far outweighed by those from Scandinavia.

WHAT TO SEE AND DO: Surprisingly there are several interesting things for visitors to do in Svolvær if they decide to explore on their own. Cruise ship companies offer different local tours and visits to nearby fishing villages, and your own offering will depend upon which line you are with. But for those on there own, here are my recommendations:

* Lofoten Krigsminnemuseum - Located along the main waterfront quay in Svolvær, this museum does provide a rather graphic picture of life in this remote coastal location during World War II and the Nazi occupation. The collection of artifacts and the displays are both outstanding and offer a reminder of what Norwegians experienced during the long occupation. It is a highlight not to be missed.

* Lofoten Explorer is a company on the waterfront that offers a variety of rib boat excursions into the surrounding waters. There are those tours that focus upon having a wildlife and landscape experience while others are oriented toward fishing. In either case, you will find their tours or fishing trips to be a great way to explore the immediate island vicinity.

* Tjeldbergtind Hike - This is an interesting, but moderately steep hiking trail leading out of the town from the intersection of the main highway (E10) and Kongsvatnveien that will take you up to a panoramic overview point where you can grasp the total surrounding of Svolvær.

* Artist galleries and craft shops - Located in the town center, there are a few very good galleries selling the work of local painters and photographers who are very good at capturing the distinct light that is a major draw in the Lofoten Islands.

DINING OUT: There are only a handful of restaurants in Svolvær that are open during the lunch period. The majority of ship passengers always seem to prefer to return to the ship to dine, which I personally believe is a mistake. The seafood is so good in Norway, as are the desserts, so those who do not sample local cuisine are missing one of the pleasures of the cruise. Here are my recommendations for a good Norwegian lunch in Svolvær:

* Bacalao - Located right on the main waterfront and it name is boldly written so you cannot miss it. The restaurant is open from 10 AM to 1 AM daily. Lunch is often busy, but if you go around 2 PM, it is quieter. Fresh fish and seafood along with traditional reconstituted dried cod known as bacalao are featured. And a more commonplace English fish and chips dish is also available. And as is true in Norway, dessert is also worth looking into.

* Du Verden is located at Torget 15 on the waterfront. It offers a more diverse menu apart from just fish and seafood. And it also provides a good dessert selection. Service can sometimes be a bit slow, especially when busy, but it is best to go for lunch around 2 PM.

* Restaurant Kloekkenet is located at Lamholmen on the waterfront. It provides a diverse lunch menu that of course features the sea, but also offers meat entrees. Their soups are thick and creamy, they often have crab cakes as an appetizer and of course serve the freshest of fish. Service is generally excellent. Some guests complain that prices are relatively high, but the old expression saying you get what you pay for does hold true. In true Norwegian tradition, butter and cream are widely used so if you are watching cholesterol, you need to pick less traditional items.

I hope that if your itinerary includes Svolvær that the old Norse gods will be kind an enable your visit by keeping the sea nice and calm.

Map of the town of Svolvær (© OpenStreetMap contributors)

Along the shoreline of Austvågøya Island

The high mountains of Austvågøya Island

The beautiful waters of Vaterfjord

The beauty of Austnestfjord (Work of Hesse 1309, GNU 1.2, Wikimedia.org)

Looking down on Svolvær from the Tjeldbergtind Trail (Work of ashfay, CC BY SA 2.0, Wikimedia.org)

The harbor at Svolvær (Work of Vincent van Zeijst, CC BY SDA 3.0, Wikimedia.org)

Coming into dock at Svolvær (Work of Zairon, CC BY SA 3.0, Wikimedia.org)

A good view of the main church rising above Svolvær

HARSTAD

Map of greater Harstad area (© OpenStreetMap contributors)

Harstad is the largest and most important town in the northern Lofoten Islands, situated on the island of Hinnøya. It is a major port and fishing oriented community with a population of nearly 24,000, making it a significant stop for cruise ships traveling into the far northern fjord region.

Harstad is located on the eastern side of Hinnøya Island, facing what has now become a narrow channel known as the Tjeldsundet, between the mainland and the Lofoten Islands. Thus it is in a very sheltered location with regard to the blustery storms that blow in from the North Sea. The city is connected to the mainland by way of the Tjeldsund Bridge that is located just southeast of the city center. The climatic patterns show a relative mildness despite Harstad being above the Arctic Circle, this being the result of the Gulf Stream that moderates the coastal environments while inland winters are quite severe. And during summer there is a period of over six weeks when there are 24 hours of perpetual daylight. However, in winter the same amount of permanent darkness makes up for the summer sun.

Hinnøya Island is quite mountainous and the highest peak in the immediate vicinity of the city center is 1,095 meters or 3,593 feet above sea level. The surrounding forests are quite thick and provide a beautiful backdrop for the city, offering its residents and visitors a variety of recreational activities.

HARSTAD HISTORY: The Harstad area has a long history of settlement that dates back over 3,000 years, well before the rise of the Vikings. By the time of the Viking golden age, Harstad was an important community and in the 15th century it was the seat of the most northern extent of Christian teaching, as its small church at Trondenes was at the outer limit of the Christian world.

Throughout its long history, Harstad was oriented both toward fishing and also as the trade center for the northern end of the Lofoten Islands and the adjacent mainland. There is also a significant amount of agriculture practiced in the vicinity of Harstad, as the climate is excellent for raising root crops, hearty grains and dairy cattle. Local craftsmen have developed a reputation for building small fishing and transport vessels, adding to the overall economic picture. Today Harstad, like many other small cities along the Norwegian coast, participates in the servicing of oil drilling platforms as well as maintenance and repair of vessels servicing the industry. And it is headquarters for new exploration by Statoil, Norway's government controlled oil company.

Tourism is limited, as few foreign tourists other than cruise passengers add to the overall economic market. However, with the bridge connecting Harstad to the mainland, more people are likely to venture out to the Lofoten Islands given their magnificent scenery and summertime recreational potential. As a cruise passenger you will find the people of Harstad very welcoming, and depending upon what activities your cruise line plans if stopping here, the day can be quite memorable.

SIGHTSEEING IN HARSTAD: Most cruise lines that stop in Harstad will offer a minimum of a half day tour around the city to show you the major sights. I highly recommend this tour because the various venues are spread out over several kilometers, and walking as a means of covering all the basics is rather intensive. There are also very few taxis or private cars and drivers available. The primary highlights include:
* Trondenes Church - This medieval church dating back as early as the 15th century is just a few kilometers from the town center on the northern margins, but a bit far to walk. The church is a stunning example of early medieval architecture with both the interior and exterior offering excellent photo

opportunities. Services and weddings still take place and perhaps you will be there when an event is taking place. If this is the case, please be respectful and you will be welcomed.

* Trondenes Historical Center is located adjacent to the church and is also a must see venue. It is adjacent to the church and will provide you with a good historical overview of the city and its surroundings. It is open daily so you should plan to visit before or after touring the church

* Trondenes Fort and Adlof Guns sitting above the city of Harstad is a must see for anyone who has an interest in local World War II history. The guns, which were a threat to any navigation of the inside passage, were quite massive and show you the power that Nazi forces brought to protect their interests while holding Norway.

These are the three major venues that should be seen while visiting Harstad. Depending upon the offerings of your cruise line, there could be more outdoor activities offered such as a mountain hike or drives to view the countryside and the interior passage.

DINING OUT: If your port call is sufficiently long or stays into the evening hours, I would strongly urge you to partake of lunch or dinner. Harstad may be a very small city, but its few excellent restaurants do offer outstanding examples of traditional Norwegian cuisine, especially fresh fish and seafood. My recommendations are:

* De 4 Roser is said by many to be the finest restaurant in northern Norway. I do not know if I would go that far, but it does offer delicious food and very friendly service that is truly hard to beat. Located at Torvey # 7A and open from 10 AM to 2 PM you will not go wrong with its fresh fish, cold salads and other local delicacies such as elk or duck.

* Umami is another highly rated and popular restaurant serving outstandingly prepared food in a very comfortable atmosphere with excellent service. It is open only for dinner from 5 PM to Midnight and it will only be possible for you to dine here if your ship is leaving in the later evening. It is located at Havnegata #23A on the waterfront.

* Bark Spiseri Og Bar As is a very excellent restaurant for lunch or dinner. It is located at Rikard Kaarboes Gate #6 on the waterfront and open from 10 AM to 3:30 AM. The only complaint is that this is not a cozy restaurant. It is often quite crowded and can be a bit loud, but that does not take away much from its very fine traditional Norwegian cuisine at reasonable prices. Their fish and fresh halibut are among the most favored specialties during summer.

A map of Harstad (© OpenStreetMap contributors)

A view of central Harstad from the deck of the ship

Even the city center of Harstad is quite hilly

For its population Harstad's waterfront seems quite cosmopolitan

A cold and rainy day in central Harstad

In early summer people's thoughts turn to gardening in Harstad

TROMSØ

A map of greater Tromsø (© OpenStreetMap contributors)

Tromsø is the largest city in Arctic Norway. Geographically it is farther north in latitude than Murmansk, Russia, thus making Tromsø the largest city in the world at such a northerly latitude. The metro population is just under 100,000 with around 75,000 within the city proper.

The geographic setting for Tromsø is in itself rather unique in that the bulk of the city occupies an elongated and rugged island known as Tromsøya in the middle of the inside passage. Its suburbs spill over onto the narrow shorelines to both the mainland side on the east and to Kvaløya Island side on the west, connected to each by a graceful suspension bridge. There is also a tunnel connecting the city to the mainland side.

Not only is Tromsø the region's largest city, but it is also rather sophisticated in that the performing arts are very well integrated into the social life and during the summer days there are numerous important musical and artistic events. The city also presents a rather urban face that visitors are surprised to see. Modern buildings, including a few moderate size high-rises vie with two to three hundred year old wood houses that date back to when all of northern Norway was still considered to be quite provincial and isolated. Thus the mix of modernity and traditional Norwegian design intermingles as if the styles were mated, giving Tromsø a very distinct architectural matrix.

HISTORIC SKETCH: Tromsø is an old city, and its surroundings are even older with evidence from archaeological sites showing it had pre Norse settlers at the time of the last glacial retreat.

By the 9th century, the Tromsø area was a meeting zone between the northern most Norse tribes and the southernmost Sámi, those we often call the Lapplanders. The actual town of Tromsø dates back to the construction of the first Christian church between 1240 and 1250, believed to have been the first church built in such far northern latitudes. The city was more of a frontier outpost rather than much of a settled community. But it served as a military and diplomatic buffer between Norway, mainly to the south and Russia primarily to the East. As Norwegian power in the region increased, Russian influence waned and by the year 1794 Tromsø received its charter as a city. It became an important trade center with the crown's permission for cod fishing to develop, and also it served as the gateway for explorations and hunting parties traveling farther north and east into the interior. Yet it was a cultural outpost of Norwegian and Germanic civilization.

By the early 1800's, hunting for whales and seals in the Arctic Ocean, exploiting them for oil, meat and hides, Tromsø became a very significant port and also a center for shipbuilding. This enabled Tromsø to develop the amenities of a real city with proper schools, churches, shops and restaurants. By 1850, it was the largest city anywhere in the Arctic.

The arrival of the 20th century saw the city replete with its own museum, a small college, several hotels and even its own brewery. The city prospered and grew in the early 20th century. Then in 1940, Norway was invaded by Nazi troops. At first Tromsø was far enough north to have not been under occupation and even briefly served as the center of the government in exile. And it also became the command center for Norwegian General Carl Gustav who attempted to mount a counter offensive against the German advance, but they proved to be too strong and eventually conquered the entire country. Tromsø was ultimately under occupation, but the city was not bombed even though the great German battleship Tirpitz was attacked and ultimately sunk by allied aircraft south of the urban area. After Norwegian liberation, there was a major flood of people into Tromsø from the far north where the Germans had devastated the countryside because of their fear that Red Army forces would advance across from Murmansk and drive them out.

Tromsø has continued to prosper through the late 20th century and into the first decades of the 21st century based upon the combination of oil exploration and development, fishing and timber. As the largest city of the far north, it has developed as the major center for commerce, banking, medical services and higher education. It is the only city in northern Norway to be home to a major university, which serves all of the northern districts. The city is also now an important research center with the Norwegian Polar Institute and the Northern Lights Observatory.

SIGHTSEEING: There are several interesting sights to see in and around the city of Tromsø, and each cruise line develops its own shore excursions. Most cruise lines do not stop for a lengthy visit, thus few if any offer tours out away from the immediate city area.

My recommendations for what to see in Tromsø, either on your own, or through one or more tours, includes the following:

* Northern Lights - If you happen to be doing one of the winter cruises on the Hurtigruten Line, Norway's main passenger ship line that plies the coast year around, you will find that the number one attraction in Tromsø and all along the coast is an evening viewing of the Northern Lights. Also if you are doing a late summer early fall cruise where there are at least eight hours of darkness in September, you will have a chance to witness this great spectacle. The sky is illuminated for anywhere from a few minutes to a couple of hours with a variety of filmy or wispy strands of light, mainly green, that are the result of particles of energy from the solar wind becoming caught in the earth's magnetic field. Once you have seen the Northern Lights, you will carry that memory with you. But if you come during summer, as most cruisers do, there is insufficient darkness to enable you to see the lights.

* The Polar Museum sits on the shore not far from where cruise ships dock. The building resembles a small barn and does not initially look inviting. Open daily, this museum tells the story of Tromsø and of various northern expeditions, including the famous Roald Amundsen.

* Tromsø Museum is located a bit out of town on Lars Thoringsvei #10, but worth the effort to visit. You can get there by taxi or city bus # 37 from the city center. There are excellent exhibits on the local region, the Northern Lights and the Sámi people.

* Polaria is a unique museum located on the waterfront not far from where cruise ships dock. It is open daily from 10 AM to 7 PM and worthy of a visit. From its name you can deduce that the featured exhibits relate to the high Arctic, both natural and historic. And the building itself is unique, looking like a series of concrete boxes collapsing down toward the water.

* Arctic Cathedral is the city's signature building, sitting across the fjord on a hill opposite the city center. The large "A" frame shape and beautiful stained glass windows make this an architectural gem that is worthy of a visit. And it is easy to reach across the main bridge from the city center if you are walking, taking a taxi or using the local city bus # 26 , which you can board in the city center.

* Tromsø Domkyrka is the main city church located on the Storgata # 25. It is a traditional wood church and reflects the 19th century era when everything in Tromsø was constructed of wood and lavishly decorated and painted. It is very easy to spot with its almost pink walls and spire trimmed in gray.

* Tromsø Public Library and City Archives occupy a very modern building just off of the Storgata with a commanding view across to the Arctic Church. This is a nice place to just sit and relax during your walking explorations of the city center, and you will be surprised at both the architectural design and size of this building for a city of under 100,000.

There are many adventure tours offered locally in Tromsø that vary from hiking, sailing the beautiful fjords, visiting a sled dog kennel to fishing. But these tours may or may not be included in your ship's itinerary and are too numerous and season to mention here. If adventure tours are of interest to you, I would strongly recommend you visit the Tromsø Tourist Information Office on the waterfront near the cruise dock, or visit them on line at: visittromso.no

DINING OUT: Depending upon your ship's schedule you will either have time for lunch or dinner in Tromsø. Some cruise ships arrive in the early evening and stay overnight so in that case you may be able to enjoy two meals in the city. I am listing several restaurants below, but I have limited the category to those serving traditional Norwegian cuisine:

* Emma's Drommenkjokken is located at Kirkengata # 8 in the city center and open from Noon to 10:30 PM. This traditional Norwegian restaurant has a very extensive menu with dishes served in a very pleasing manner. Fish and seafood clearly dominate, but whale and other meat dishes are also part of the menu. As starters there are herring dishes and wonderful soups, especially fish soups. And of course this being Norway you must save room for dessert.

* Mathallen is one of the city's best-known restaurants located at Gronnegata # 58/60 in the city center. It is open from 10 AM to 11 PM with continuous service. They do offer a tasting menu that gives you samples of a variety of dishes. Specialties include fish, seafood, reindeer and even unique dishes such as a fish burger. You will not be disappointed.

* Bardus Bistro is located at Cora Sandeis gate # 4 in the city center and an easy walk from the ship. It is open from Noon to 11 PM with continuous

service. Once again the theme is traditional Norwegian cuisine with outstanding fish soups, fresh cod and salmon and reindeer stew. The atmosphere has a bit of a pub like flavor, but the food is very traditional and outstandingly prepared.

* Art Cafe is located in the city center at Richard Withs Plass # 2 and open from 11 AM to 10 PM. It is a very beautiful restaurant with an artistic atmosphere as the name implies. In traditional Norwegian style, you get the feel you are eating in someone's home. Their soups, main dishes and desserts are all excellent.

With Tromsø being quite a significant city there are dozens more restaurants in the city center with easy access to and from the ship. I have only chosen those that I thought best represented the Norwegian tradition. But for anyone longing for a burger and fries, pizza or other more non-traditional foods, you will find Tromsø sure to please.

The dramatic beauty of Tromsøfjorden

The lighting and mood around Tromsø changes every few minutes

The mainland shoreline suburbs of Tromsø

The city center skyline of Tromsø from the ship

Residential Tromsø on the island is very hilly

Old 19th century wood buildings along the Storgata

The Storgata is the old main pedestrian street of the city

Parts of central Tromsø have a strong urban flavor

The Tromsø cultural and music center

The Tromsø Domkyrka is a traditional wood structure

A late afternoon view of the Arctic Church

The unique architecture of Polaria

An inviting park bench in residential Tromsø

ALTA

The surroundings of Alta, Norway (© OpenStreetMap contributors)

Alta is one of those lesser ports that in all likelihood you will not visit. Only a few of the more upmarket cruise lines along with the local Hurtigruten ships call in at Alta. The surrounding fjord country is noted for its magnificent scenery, but the town is quite small and does not really offer any significant tourist services, especially for the larger cruise vessels. Alta has less than 7,000 permanent residents and it is located away from the open sea on a very protected fjord. Because the town is sheltered, the winter climate is not as harsh as locations closer to the open sea. Although well into the high Arctic, the sheltered location means that around Alta and in the valley to the south there is little or no permafrost. And rather than being in a bare tundra environment the hillsides around Alta are covered with groves of birch trees. Winters are cold and bleak, but the short three month summer is somewhat mild with temperatures around 10 degrees Celsius, which is approximately 52 degrees Fahrenheit. Because of the sheltering effect of the fjord, Alta does not receive heavy snowfall, but there is a permanent snow cover for about five to six months.

With the air being relatively clear and there being a lower frequency of storms or cloud cover, Alta has become one of the prime viewing sites in which to enjoy the spectacular displays of the Northern Lights.

The Altaelva River flows through a rather peaceful and beautiful valley before emptying into the Altafjorden. Farther up river from Alta is Sautso Canyon, a rather magnificent gorge carved through soft rock by the river. It is said to be one of the deepest canyons in Europe. Again some cruise lines may offer a short tour to visit the river and its spectacular gorge.

There was a major controversy that brewed up in 1979 when the government wanted to build a hydroelectric dam and power plant south of the town. Locals fought the move, but the government ultimately prevailed. The argument was that the building of the dam would curtail the spawning of salmon, which are a big part of the local economy. But fortunately measures were taken to mitigate the impact and this is still considered to be a prime salmon fishing location.

A BRIEF LOCAL HISTORY: The earliest inhabitants in the Alta region can be dated back over 6,200 years. Little is known about how they lived other than that they were primarily hunters living at the edge of the last of the glacial ice. They did leave an artistic record in the form of some carvings on the exposed rock that are today protected as a UNESCO World Heritage Site. This site at Hjemmeluft is easily visited from the town of Alta and some cruise itineraries do offer a tour.

Until the start of the 20th century, tensions existed between the local Sámi tribe and the Norwegian settlers, the origins going back to mistrust since the earliest settlement. Today the migratory Sámi with their reindeer herds are more readily accepted.

Today's town of Alta has the appearance of a modern, well-planned community and bears little resemblance to the earlier village. This is because the town suffered a catastrophic fire at the close of World War II. What keeps such an isolate town functioning? That is a fair question that people often ask when they see where Alta is located. It is the major trade center for the northern region of Finnmark. And it also is home to Finnmark University College, the most northerly institution of higher learning in the country. During winter, an ice hotel offering luxurious accommodation is created for those few winter visitors that come primarily for the Northern Lights.

SIGHTS TO SEE: There are only a handful of specific sites or activities in Alta worthy of note. These include:

* Northern Lights Observatory for those who will brave the cold and dark of winter to come and see this spectacular sight. For those of you coming in the very late summer or early fall on the few remaining cruises, you may have a chance to observe the Northern Lights, but it is essentially a mid winter experience.

* Alta Museum located at Altaveien # 19 on the edge of town is open from 11 AM to 4 PM daily. Its primary feature is the collection of rock carvings that have been given UNESCO World Heritage Site status. You will either need to come by taxi or take the tour from your ship if it is offered.

* Tirpitz Museum is located along Kafjord about a 40 minute drive outside of Alta. It is open from 10 AM to 9 PM and is worth visiting if you have a tour offered or can find a local taxi. This small museum is filled with Tirpitz memorabilia and is located not far from where the great battleship was attacked.

DINING OUT: There are a few restaurants in the main town of Alta that offer lunch with a Norwegian flair. In the event you have time for lunch and do not wish to return to the ship, here are my suggestions:

* Restaurant Haldde in the Thon Hotel Vica at Fogdebakkan #6 is open for lunch and dinner. It is a good restaurant by Alta standards, but a bit over priced for what it offers. Lunch and dinner hours can be rather busy, but if you are patient you will find that their lunch selection will include a variety of fish and seafood dishes, and this far north, reindeer meat is the main red meat you will find. Good desserts are a part of the restaurant's offerings.

* Du Verden Matbar is located at Markedsgata #21-25 and is open from 11 AM to 11:30 PM. This is a good restaurant for lunch or dinner and is very popular with locals. Stockfish and reindeer are of course house specialties, but they also offer vegetarian dishes. You will find the food and service comparable to what you would expect in a major city.

Remember that Alta is a small community and choices for restaurants at lunch are rather limited when it comes to good, traditional cuisine.

The prehistoric rock art of Alta (Work of Vulcano, CC BY SA 4.0, Wikimedia.org)

The Altaleva River has carved one of Europe's deepest canyons (Work of Sami Keinanen, CC BY SA 2.0, Wikimedia.org)

The cold waters of the Altaleva River south of Alta

The Altaleva Valley south of the town of Alta

Over the rooftops of the modern town center of Alta

On the main shopping street in Alta (Work of Andreas Haldorsen, CC BY SA 2.0, Wikimedia.org)

HAMMERFEST

A map of greater Hammerfest (© OpenStreetMap contributors)

Hammerfest is located in the very far northern reaches of Norway, a short distance south of where the Arctic and North Atlantic Oceans meet. The city occupies the northern end of the island of Kvaløya, which is connected to the mainland by a bridge. The city is built around a deep water harbor and has unrestricted access to the open ocean and the main shipping routes between the Russian Arctic and the rest of Europe. The island is protected from the brunt of winter storms off the ocean by the mountainous island of Sørøya, but this island does not block access to the northwest opening into the ocean.

This far north one would expect a brutally cold winter climate, but surprisingly because of the Gulf Stream, Hammerfest receives a mix of rain, sleet and snow with temperatures not drastically below freezing. However, when it snows, the amounts at times can be exceptionally heavy and this poses an avalanche danger since the surrounding rocky hillsides are bare of trees. The weather is essentially harsh, but not as brutal as it would be inland. Summers are cool, damp and often cloudy or foggy. There are swings between having approximately six weeks of total daylight in summer and then the reverse in winter, with days on either end of the daylight or darkness where only a few minutes to a couple of hours of daylight or darkness occur. The landscape at this latitude and with the exposure to winds from the open sea is definitely described as tundra. There are very few trees capable of growing under such conditions.

A FASCINATING HISTORY: Hammerfest as a town only dates back to 1789 when it was granted trade rights in the far north by King Christian VII or Denmark. Prior to being given those rights, the harbor was used for fishing boats to take shelter. It was also used as a base for high Arctic expeditions to hunt for fur bearing seals and for whaling. It became a town in 1838 with regard to establishing its charter.

One would not have expected the Napoleonic Wars to have an impact upon Norway, especially not a town as far north as Hammerfest, but surprisingly it did. Norway was under Danish rule and Denmark did participate in the war on the side of Napoleon. Because Hammerfest was the major trade center for the rich fishing and Arctic hunting waters of the high Arctic, the British blockaded the coast and it was only a matter of time before their ships would attack the town. In July 1809, two British warships attacked Hammerfest, which was defended by two cannons. The battle lasted for over one hour, but ended when the Hammerfest batteries depleted their ammunition. The British proceeded to loot was the Hammerfest locals had not been able to cart away before the British came ashore. Following the British departure, Hammerfest was established as a garrison, as prior it was locals that had manned the batteries, and they were not either well equipped or trained, and yet had been able to inflict some casualties upon the British. To this day, the story of the role of Hammerfest in the Napoleonic Wars is still taught with great pride.

Hammerfest had to be partially rebuilt after the great 1890 fire that had destroyed much of the community, which like most Norwegian towns, was built primarily of wood. But in the case of the reconstruction, a good portion of the funds raised came from Kaiser Wilhelm II of Germany because of his prior visits on his royal yacht and his affection for the town and its people.

During World War II, Hammerfest became a major Nazi base because it was very close to the Allied shipping lanes where supplies were being convoyed to Murmansk to help the Soviet Union in fighting the German invasion. Unlike the defenses the Norwegians had in place after the Napoleonic Wars, the Nazi made Hammerfest almost impregnable with the coastal and inland batteries they established. To attempt to hamper Allied shipping, the German U-boat was the main weapon of choice, and given its proximity to the shipping lanes, Hammerfest became a very strategic submarine base. Hammerfest paid a terrible price because it had become such an important German base of operations. The Soviet Air Force bombed Hammerfest in early 1944 and again in late summer of the same year. Although this did significant damage, the Germans evacuated all of the local residents when the Red Army began to press its invasion into the eastern margins of Finnmark. To hamper the Russian onslaught, the Germans systematically looted and burned all of the towns and villages, including Hammerfest. The destruction to the community and local infrastructure was essentially total, unlike any other damage inflicted either by the retreating Germans or allied forces anywhere else in Norway.

Following the war, the entire community of Hammerfest and all of the surrounding villages had to be totally rebuilt. But the Norwegians were determined to remove the battle damage, which they did. Today there is the Reconstruction Museum in Hammerfest, which tells the story of the destruction and resurrection of the town, and it is a major attraction.

Today Hammerfest is profiting from the new liquefied natural gas plant at Snøhvit, which will stimulate the economy with the addition of many well paying jobs. Tourism is a growing part of the economic scene because of the increased interest in recreational fishing. There is also a daily tour boat that takes visitors around Nordkapp, known in English as North Cape, the northernmost point of land in Europe. There is also a significant glacier close by on the mainland that is the most northerly such feature on the continent. The town also serves as a local trade center, especially for the Sámi who keep significant herds of reindeer on Mageroya and Kvaløya Island for the summer. The reindeer have the run of both islands, and in Hammerfest they often come right into the town to graze on people's flowerbeds or vegetable gardens. It may sound charming, but the local residents find it disruptive as well as unsanitary having so many animals wandering through their yards and gardens.

Mageroya is also the home to North Cape, which is visited during summer by numerous cruise ships. Many cruise liners now do stop in Hammerfest for a few hours, but often not long enough for any tours into the more rugged interior.

LOCAL SIGHTS TO SEE: There are few venues of any great significance in Hammerfest. The overall flavor of the town, which encircles the bay is interesting because of its colorful houses that seem to take the place of having lush vegetation. Just seeing a significant town of around 10,000 in a bleak tundra environment is in itself interesting. The major sights in Hammerfest include:

* Museum of Reconstruction for Finnmark and Northern Troms is located at Kirkegata #21 adjacent to the town's main church. It is open daily and is considered the major attraction. The exhibits and artifacts tell of the Nazi forced evacuation and subsequent destruction of the towns in the region. And it portrays the heroism of the people and their determination to rebuild.
* Polar Bear Society is located on Hamnegata # 3, which is on the waterfront. The museum is only open from 10 AM to 2 PM, but it is a must see venue. Although there are no polar bears in Norway proper, they are major on Svalbard Island off the north coast, west from Hammerfest. And they have figured greatly into Norwegian explorations of the far north. The museum is always a big hit with visitors because of all the mystique surrounding the Polar Bear.
* Struve Geodetic Arc is a monument located around the harbor from the town center, but often cruise ships dock on this side of the harbor making the monument a short walk away. Over 100 years ago a Russian scientist named Friedrich Struve led a team that measured an arc of longitude from Hammerfest south to the Black Sea in an attempt to better calculate the earth's radius and determine its overall size. This project was accomplished long before computers or scientific equipment and is an amazing feat, which has earned the site UNESCO World Heritage Site status.
* Hammerfest Town Center with its mother and child fountain is a pleasant place to sit for a while and simply watch the people about their daily activities. The fountain is quite charming and is the focus of the town center.
* Hammerfest Church located on Kirkegata # 21 is a new post World War II construct, but built in the delightful manner of local wood churches around the country. It is quite tastefully decorated and reflects true Norwegian sensibilities regarding decorum.

DINING OUT: There are few restaurants overall in Hammerfest and depending upon your itinerary you many not have time for lunch. However, if you are fortunate enough to stay for a few hours and would like to sample some traditional cuisine, I have the following two recommendations:
* Qa spiseri is in the center of town at Sjogata #8 and open daily for lunch and dinner. It is far from elegant, simply a rather ordinary restaurant serving basic local fare. It is popular with the local community and I have never heard any serious complaints from returning guests once onboard ship. As is expected, fish soup, fish and reindeer are on the menu, all nicely prepared.
* Havorna Restaurant is in the harbor area at Strandgata #16 and open for lunch and dinner. This restaurant is quite small and is included with the local fish market, thus it sometimes can be too full to accommodate visitors. The menu is rather basic and again fish soup, seasonal fish and whale meat dishes are the mainstay.

There are a few other restaurants in Hammerfest, but the specialties are either sushi, Chinese food or pizza. There are only the two choices above for a lunch that would have any degree of Norwegian flair.

A map of Hammerfest (© OpenStreetMap contributors)

The Hammerfest Harbor (Work of Clemensfranz, CC BY SA 3.0, Wikimedia.org)

Large cruise ships often dock across from the town center (Work of Balou46, CC BY SA 4.0, Wikimedia.org)

The attractive Hammerfest church (Work of Balou46, CC BY SA 4.0, Wikimedia.org)

The Hammerfest Reconstruction Museum

The city's reindeer problem (Work of Manxruler, CC BY SA 3.0, Wikimedia.org)

HONNINGSVÅG AND NORDKAPP

Magerøya Island is the most northerly island in Norway, facing out onto the Barents Sea, which is part of the Arctic Ocean. The only significant town on this large island, which is connected by tunnel to the mainland, is Honningsvåg, the port of call for visits to Nordkapp, known in English as North Cape, the very northernmost tip of Europe. Honningsvåg has the distinction of being the most northerly city in Norway, but only by a bit of political slight of hand. The Norwegian government legislated that to have the designation of being a city, the population must be over 5,000. Honningsvåg only has about 2,400 residents, but it received its city status one year before the new legislation went into effect in 1997. A special waiver was given so that it would not loose its recognition as the most northerly "city" in the country.

Honningsvåg is located on a deep water bay that is quite sheltered from storms, situated on the island's south coast, just across a relatively narrow channel from the mainland. North Cape, which is the object of the port call is located atop a high set of cliffs facing the stormy waters of the Arctic Ocean, a drive of approximately one hour across the island. But it gives visitors an opportunity to see a true tundra landscape and also catch sight of thousands of reindeer during their summer grazing. These reindeer belong to Sámi families who drive them overland and then rely upon the Norwegian Army to ferry them across to their summer grazing each spring. After fattening up with spring and summer grazing, they are able to swim back to the mainland and are then taken to more sheltered areas. But they are allowed to graze freely across the island for the warmer months.

THINGS TO DO IN HONNINGSVÅG: There is little for the visitor to see in Honningsvåg, as it is strictly a fishing and local service center. But either before or after taking a tour to North Cape, a walk through town does give you a chance to capture the flavor of living on the tundra in such a northerly location. Winter would be quite extreme, both cold and continuously dark for over six or seven weeks. This is the quiet time when little happens in Honningsvåg, but they do receive Hurtigruten ships that bring passengers who want to come and experience the Northern Lights.

* Nordkappmusset is located on the waterfront at Holmen #1 and is open only from Noon to 4 PM. It does offer various exhibits on the importance of North Cape, the fishing industry of Honningsvåg and the Nazi occupation of the town during World War II. Although small, the museum is well organized and worth your effort to visit.

* Perloportenkulturhus located in town at Storgata # 19 is an interesting place to see a short live presentation called "Our Northernmost Life." This show

with local talent gives you a feel for the culture of the region and a taste of what life is like in Europe's most northerly city. Upon arrival, you can check with the visitor's center or ask anyone in town what time the show will be put on.

VISITING NORDKAPP: Most visitors will book their ship's motor coach tour to Nordkapp (North Cape,) as this is the major highlight of visiting Honningsvåg. The drive will take about an hour during which time you will see both the rugged nature of the island of Magerøya and the importance of its tundra vegetation as food for thousands of reindeer. During early summer there will still be snow on the ground in partial cover

The Visitor's Center at Nordkapp is an impressive multi-level building that extends down the cliff face. It contains a restaurant, cafe, gift shop and theater where special presentations are shown. And the windows present panoramic sweeping views out over the cape and the Arctic Ocean. There is an outdoor promenade leading right to the cliff's edge, but protected by guardrails. If the weather is tolerable, you can enjoy the impact of the cape while being out of doors.

Actually Nordkapp is not the most northerly point, as guides will note. There is one cape to the west that is just a few meters farther north, but because of the broken topography it is inaccessible and thus Nordkapp became officially recognized as the most northerly point in Europe.

DINING OUT: Dining in Honningsvåg is exceptionally limited at lunchtime. But if you are going on the tour to Nordkapp, the visitor's center there does have both a restaurant and snack bar where you can have anything from a full meal to something light to satisfy until you return to your ship.

The only truly nice restaurant in Honningsvåg that does regularly serve lunch is the Corner Spicerie located on Fiskeriveien # 2A and open from 10 AM to 11 PM. The menu includes fish, especially cod, shellfish such as crab and also a selection of burgers. The quality is very good and the service is friendly, but often a bit slow if the restaurant is crowded. You will be surprised by such a nice restaurant in this small of a community.

Docking in Honningsvåg

The colorful harbor of Honningsvåg

Honningsvåg is rather bleak in its tundra environment

The tundra landscape of Magerøya with its summer reindeer herds

There are a few Sámi camps on Magerøya

The Nordkapp Visitor's Center

The outdoor Nordcaoo Monument

Sailing under Nordkapp en route to Russia

CRUISING TO MURMANSK AND ARKHANGELSK, RUSSIA

The far northwest of Russia (© OpenStreetMap contributors)

For those of you whose cruise itinerary will include a visit to Murmansk and possibly beyond to Arkhangelsk in Russia's far northern lands, this chapter will be of great value. Apart from having been to Russia 42 times, I have also had the good fortune to explore this high Arctic region of far northwestern Russia. Speaking the language was a big help, as I was able to gain an insight into the lives of the people living in a region that is climatically quite severe by the standards most of us are accustomed to. No two cities in a similar environment could be as different. Murmansk is a 20th century creation that grew into a major port serving the Communist government of the Soviet Union. Arkhangelsk is a very old city whose roots go back to pioneers and missionaries that settled back in the 12th century, thus it has deep Russian roots.

IMPORTANT THINGS TO KNOW ABOUT VISITING RUSSIA: The Russian government is rather strict with regard to entry into and exit from the country. Most visitors will need a visa from the Russian authorities if they want to have the freedom to sightsee on their own. Only a handful of countries are exempt where their governments and Russia have mutual agreements regarding travel. Citizens with passports from Argentina, Brazil, Chile, China,

Hong Kong, Israel, Kazakhstan names a few nations whose passport holders do not need visas.

If you do not have a visa, you may still leave the ship and participate in sightseeing activities that are organized by your cruise line or by tour companies that are authorized to provide you with temporary visas for each activity away from the ship. If you choose this more private alternative, make certain the company has the authority to provide you with the temporary permit to leave the ship. At all times when not on an official sightseeing tour, you must stay onboard the ship.

Many cruise lines do offer private cars with drivers and guides to enable you to have flexibility in sightseeing where you are not part of an organized group. Such arrangements can be made through your ship's shore excursion office.

If you have a visa and go off on your own, you will find that very few people are able to speak English or other European languages. And most of the signs and informational posts are written in the Cyrillic Alphabet, so getting around would be difficult.

Credit cards can be used in most shops and restaurants, but if you are going out on your own or with a private car and driver and guide you should carry some Russian roubles, as foreign currencies are not accepted in Russia.

If you have a chance to speak with your guide or other Russians regarding their lives or their views, do not be forward in pressing them for opinions of a political nature. Most Russian people are very proud of their heritage, their country and the fact that it has emerged from its long Soviet Era. Many of us who live in the West have very strong views regarding the Russian government and the country's current president that are often rather negative. What you do not want to do is get into an argument over political or global issues when you are a visitor in their country. Even if they voice negative views, which on occasion some will do, it is best to try and remain neutral in your demeanor. Be the polite and correct visitor and in the end you will leave with pleasant memories, as Russians are very warm and giving people.

MURMANSK

The city of Murmansk is one of the two most important warm water ports in all of Russia. A map of the country will show you that despite having a very long Arctic and Pacific coastline, the northern latitudes mean that much of it is locked in ice for many months of the year, although the winter period is changing with global warming. Murmansk benefits from being at the far northern end of the Gulf Stream, that important warm water current that comes across from the tropical waters of North America, washes the coast of Norway and reaches Murmansk. Russia's other warm water port is Vladivostok, which is thousands of miles to the east on the Pacific Coast close to the borders of China and North Korea. Thus Murmansk is a critical port for commercial and military uses because it is due north of the Russian heartland west of the Ural Mountains.

The landscape is one of moderately hilly ground that is covered in a mix of tundra vegetation interspersed with groves of willow, birch and spruce, which are outliers of the dense coniferous taiga to the south. The climate is essentially continental with severely cold and snowy winters. There are 138 days each winter in which some snow will fall. And record low temperatures have almost reached minus 40 degrees Celsius/Fahrenheit. And at its high latitude above the Arctic Circle, Murmansk experiences six to eight weeks of absolute total darkness each winter. With a population of over 400,000, it is the world's largest city at such a high latitude.

HISTORY OF MURMANSK: Murmansk is a young city founded in 1915 because of the pressing need for a warm water port during World War I. The building of a railroad line was the key factor and Murmansk was the northern terminus because of its deep and sheltered harbor. Officially it was the last city to be granted a charter in 1916 by Tsar Nicholas II just less than one year before he would be forced to abdicate the throne. The original name was Romanov-on-Murman, but in April 1917 the name was changed to Murmansk, as the Tsar was now no longer head of state.

In October 1917, the Bolshevik Revolution occurred in which Communist forces took control of the government in St. Petersburg. This precipitated a civil war between the Communist Red Army forces and the White Army that was loyal to the tsar and imperial family. A British naval squadron occupied the harbor and city until 1920, supporting the White Army forces in their fight to oust the Communists from the government.

By 1922, most of the country was in the hands of the Red Army and the Union of Soviet Socialist Republics was proclaimed in December 1922. Murmansk ultimately became a part of the Soviet Union and by 1926 it had its own city soviet council. The city quickly grew, as the Soviet Union industrialized under the rule of Joseph Stalin, its warm water port being critical. But its role would heighten with the outbreak of World War II.

After Nazi Germany invaded Russia and blockaded Leningrad (formerly St. Petersburg), the import of war materials, food and other vital supplies was critical to the nation's survival. The Allies organized convoys to supply the Soviets through Murmansk, and this in part is why Nazi forces considered Norway to be such a vital link since its ports could shelter U-boats that would prey upon the Allied convoys.

German forces attempted to cut off the vital supply route, using Finland as a staging area. The Finns had given permission for Nazi troops to be stationed on their soil because the Red Army had made an attempt to recapture Finland, claiming that their 1917 independence was not valid and that they were a part of old Imperial Russia. The combination of winter weather and very stiff Red Army resistance made the capture of Murmansk impossible, but the city did suffer from severe enemy shelling that destroyed much of its vital infrastructure. Like Leningrad, Stalingrad, Minsk, Kiev and many other cities in the country, Murmansk was proclaimed a Heroic City by the government following the war.

Following World War II, the Soviet Union and the West became embroiled in the Cold War that essentially lasted until the fall of the Soviet system in 1991. Murmansk retained its strong military role, especially as a submarine base and also an Arctic research center given that Canada and the United States lay over the northern horizon. Today Murmansk is still the most important submarine port in all of Russia even though the Cold War is essentially over.

The city is filled with memorials and statues to the heroes of World Wars I and II and also the Russian Civil War. It is a city where you can feel its military significance when your tour its important sites. But most dominant of all is Alyosha, a giant statue of a soldier in a trench coat that stands 35.5 meters or 116 feet high, perched atop a hill overlooking the city. This has become a sacred site for Russians who have strong memories passed down from generation to generation with regard to World War II. Alyosha is pivotal in that remembrance.

THINGS TO SEE AND DO: Although I will be listing the important historic and scenic attractions, most of you will have little choice as to what you will see unless you either have a visa or hire a private car and driver/guide. The tours will have a predetermined itinerary that will not allow you any personalized choices. But hopefully you will get to see the majority of the places I have listed. I am not giving names or addresses because in the city they would all be written in Cyrillic, and opening hours often are not adhered to in many instances. My recommendations for Murmansk are therefore:

* Alyosha is the number one attraction, as I noted above. It is a marvelous statue and has such great significance to the Russian people. He represents all the thousands of Red Army soldiers who died in defense of their country. That is why you will see fresh flowers and wreaths at the foot of Alyosha that people bring almost daily. To reach Alyosha you must be on a group tour or have private transportation. Even if you have a visa, it is too far to walk from the city center.
* Northern Fleet Naval Museum receives mixed reviews from those who visit. The building itself is badly in need of restoration, and the exhibits are rather staid and conservative with now wow factor. But given the importance of the subject matter to the history of Murmansk, the museum does represent an important part of the city's development.
* Lenin Nuclear Ice Breaker is a very popular exhibit for most Western visitors. If you are not part of a group tour, special arrangements should be made at the time you arrange your car and driver/guide. Once again there is no wow factor, yet the ice breaker speaks for itself. It was a remarkable piece of equipment and represents a high point in Soviet Arctic exploration. The tour is conducted in Russian, but if you are part of a group or have a private guide, they will translate for you. It is one of the highlights of a visit to Murmansk.
* Fine Art Museum is not large and impressive as in St. Petersburg, but it does feature artists from the far north and the work is excellent. Russian landscape painting is done in an impressionistic style and is highly sought after in the West. The museum claims to be open from 10 AM to 5 PM except Tuesday.
* Memorial Complex to the Soldiers and Seamen Who Have Died in Peacetime is a very somber, yet elegant memorial. It shows how important honoring those who have served their country is in Russia. The memorial and its church offer a glimpse into the devotion Russians feel for personal sacrifice. Also the location gives an outstanding view out over the city.
* Murmansk Shopping Mall and Entertainment Center on Lenina Avenue is the city's major shopping and entertainment complex. Although it may not meet standards of the glitz of the West, it is important to visit because you get a feeling for the changes taking place today in Russian retailing. It shows you a different side of this rather somber city.
* Murmansk Railway Station will not be on your group tour, but if you have a personal interest in trains, I would suggest a quick visit if you are out with a private guide. This rather ornate blue and white building typifies the attention to detail given to railway stations in the Soviet Era. And like so many other cities today, it is badly in need of repair. But if a train is arriving or departing, you will find it a satisfying visit.

There are literally dozens of monuments and memorials all over the city that represent different aspects of the role of Murmansk and those stationed here in war and peacetime. Rather than fill pages with sites you may not get to see, I simply trust that your group or private guide will point out any of the monuments you pass in your journey around the city.

DINING OUT: If you are on a group tour chances are that you will be returned to the ship for lunch if it is a morning tour. Afternoon tours will depart following lunch. However, if you are out with a private car and driver, you can stop for lunch and your guide will be there to assist. Few restaurants in Murmansk will have English menus or wait staff that will speak English or other languages. Russian food is hearty and very good. You should try it and I am sure that even in Murmansk, which is far from the major cities, you will enjoy sampling the cuisine. My three recommendations are as follows:

* Stolle is located on Lenina Avenue # 97 and open all day. This is one of a popular chain of restaurants that specialize in Russian pies. But unlike what you might think of as a dessert restaurant, Russian pies are main courses. There is a great variety of meats, vegetables and yes also desserts. My favorite is a cabbage pie as the main, and then a fruit pie for dessert. It is quick, fresh and tasty and a Russian example of slow fast food.

* Mama Mia has an Italian name, but most of its menu is traditional Russian, but with a few Italian dishes. It is located on Egnorova Street # 14 and open for lunch at Noon. There are many very traditional Russian dishes on the menu and the quality is very good. And they do have an English menu. Your best choice if you want a good Russian meal, but count upon your guide to interpret the names of the different food choices.

A map of Murmansk (© OpenStreetMap contributors)

Looking over the city center and docks at Murmansk

A rooftop view over the Murmansk city center

The heroic statue of Alyosha stands over Murmansk

The eternal flame and flower offerings at the base of Alyosha

The statue of the woman waiting for her husband to return from the sea

View toward the sea from the statue of the waiting woman

Monument to heroic Poles lost at sea during World War II

A children's poster for summer activities at the Palace of Culture

Stalinist residential architecture in Murmansk

ARKHANGELSK

Unlike Murmansk, Arkhangelsk is a centuries old Russian city whose origin is from well back in early tsarist times, and with a very strong religious flavor. Located near the mouth of the Severnaya Dvina River on the White Sea, it is an far northern community, but just slightly below the Arctic Circle.

The landscape of Arkhangelsk is essentially flat to just slightly rolling and the land is right on the northern margins of the great boreal forest or taiga. Spruce, willow and birch trees dominate the countryside and the agricultural potential is severely limited by the short growing season.

The climate of Arkhangelsk is definitely continental and more like that of western Siberia, as it is too far east for the Gulf Stream to have any significant influence. Winter temperatures are well below zero Celsius, often below minus 40 degrees. And snow covers the ground for up to six months out of the year. In centuries past the major winter travel routes were the frozen rivers, and even today with global warming these ice roads are still used for several months each year. During summer, however, the rivers then served as water highways since they flow primarily north toward the Arctic Ocean. And the size and depth of the Severnaya Dvina gave Arkhangelsk its importance as a northern port dating back to medieval times.

As a city, Arkhangelsk is larger than Murmansk with approximately 420,000 residents, but being just slightly south of the Arctic Circle, it is not able to claim to be the most northerly large city in the world. That distinction does belong to Murmansk by just a few degrees of latitude. Only a handful of cruise ships venture as far east as Arkhangelsk, and if your cruise itinerary includes this ancient city, you will be fortunate. It is an architectural gem with regard to its early Russian heritage. And it is also in many ways still a frontier city.

BRIEF HISTORY: Arkhangelsk may have dated back to as early as the 9th century because of Viking chronicles that note a community near the mouth of what is now known to be the Severnaya Dvina River. A fortified monastery was built near the banks of the river and dedicated to the Archangel Michael during the 12th century by the then powerful kingdom centered upon what is today Veliky Novgorod. The actual historic founding of the city dates to 1584, when Tsar Ivan the Terrible ordered the establishment of a trade center close by and it ultimately took its name from the monastery. Trade in furs and timber in exchange for European goods became a major factor in the settlement's development. It is believed that Arkhangelsk was the first Russian port to trade directly with England. The importance of Arkhangelsk cannot be under estimated, as up until the founding of St. Petersburg and the assertion of Russian naval might, the Baltic Sea was not readily accessible to central Russia. Thus Arkhangelsk was the main trade outlet for Moscow all during the 15th and 16th centuries. It came under attack by both the Poles and Norwegians on several occasions.

After 1703 with the establishment of St. Petersburg on the Gulf of Finland, the importance of Arkhangelsk diminished and it began to decline. But there was a brief resurgence of importance during the Northern War with Sweden between which was already in progress when St. Petersburg was founded. A major fortress named Novodvinsk was begun in 1701 to add to the overall defense of the river delta and secure trade. The Swedes attacked the fortress the same year it was begun, and fortunately the Russians were able to be victorious. But this did not ultimately diminish the importance of St. Petersburg, which became the naval headquarters for the nation.

The Napoleonic Wars of the early 19th century saw Arkhangelsk serving as a vital support for supplies to reach the interior of Russia. In the mid 19th century, Arkhangelsk was connected to Moscow by rail, but it was still competing with St. Petersburg with regard to trade.

During World War I the city was a supply point and later after the Bolshevik Revolution of 1917, it became a center of resistance, held by the White Army forces. But ultimately it fell under Communist rule, as did the entire country by 1922. During World War II, the city served a vital role in helping to supply Russian forces fighting on the Eastern Front with many supplies, both military and domestic. Nazi troops had expectations of capturing Murmansk and Arkhangelsk to totally neutralize the Allied convoy assistance, but their vision fortunately never materialized.

The city is today a vital port for trade, exporting timber, fish and assorted minerals mined in the far north. It is also a center for Arctic research thanks to global warming enabling longer periods when the ocean is ice free. To keep the port open as long as possible, Russia has built some large icebreakers and this is vital to a longer trade season for Arkhangelsk.

SIGHTS TO SEE: There are many very interesting and historic sights to be seen in Arkhangelsk. However, remember the restrictions placed upon tourists by the Russian government. You must have a visa or be from one of a handful of countries visa exempt to get out on your own. The next option to having a greater degree of freedom is to arrange through your cruise line for a car, driver and guide. And finally most passengers will opt for one of the ship sponsored group tours by motor coach. The sights I am listing in this section are what I believe to be the most important in and around the city. It will depend upon what option or tour you select as to what you will be able to see during your visit to Arkhangelsk. My recommendations are:

* Chumbarova-Luchinskovo Avenue is one of the major highlights in the city center. Originally Arkhangelsk was constructed almost totally of wood. Buildings were beautifully built and highly decorated, but as the city grew into the 20th century, most were destroyed to make way for massive concrete apartment complexes. Chumbarova-Luchinskovo Avenue is a street where dozens have been preserved and today serve as restaurants, shops and museums. The street is dedicated to pedestrians only and is the true delight of modern Arkhangelsk.

* Victory War Monument and Eternal Flame pays homage to World War II and is considered to be hallowed ground by local residents. It is located along the northern embankment of the river in the center of the city and is a very major stop on all group and private tours.

* Malye Korely Open Air Museum is located about an hour drive south of the city along the river. This outdoor museum has brought together examples of the historic wood architecture of the far north. It is a grand experience given that you not only see what Arkhangelsk would have been like, but local guides and personnel dressed in traditional garb and performing various tasks make this a fascinating experience. If you go in mid summer please be sure to take with some insect repellant, as the northern mosquitos can be very pesky.

* Small Korela Wooden Architecture and Folk Art Museum is right in the city, and like the Malye Korely museum, this one also features the importance of the wood architecture that was once so commonplace all across the north country and into Siberia. This small museum is not as diverse but gives much of the same experience without traveling an hour each way between the city and Malye Korely, leaving more time to enjoy the city's other sights.

* Arkhangelsk Merchant Yards Museum is located along the river's northern embankment. This museum presents an excellent history of the city's founding and development through its many fascinating exhibits. It is open from 10 AM to 7 PM daily.

* St. Nicholas Church is in the heart of the city and a must see venue. Built in the true Russian Orthodox style over two centuries ago, it is still an active church and you may be able to stand in the back and watch and listen to the morning liturgy, which is very inspirational.

* Northern Sea Museum located in the city center is a very good museum with exhibits concerned with the close ties between Arkhangelsk and the sea. Its exhibits are well crafted, but unfortunately the descriptions are primarily written in Cyrillic and you will need a guide to interpret.

There are many monuments and statues around the city that are all of historic interest. But you will not have time to visit them all. On most group or private tours, you will see a good number in passing. Important statues include; "Papa Lenin," Peter the Great, General Kuznetsov and the Monument to Russian Wives and many more.

* Solovetsky Monastery is one of the great treasures of northern Russia. It is a UNESCO World Heritage Site and especially spectacular. Built in 1436 on Solovetsky Island in the White Sea, it is accessible by air only during a one day port call in Arkhangelsk. Not all cruise lines offer a tour, as it is expensive and very few passengers are aware of the significance of this great fortress monastery. During the Soviet Era it served as a prison and then as a labor camp and has only been restored in recent years.

DINING OUT: Most guests will not be dining out in Arkhangelsk because the majority of tours are only half day in length and then without a visa they are unable to leave the ship. For any full day tour, lunch will be included but the restaurant of choice will be predetermined. Only if you have a visa, are able to leave the ship without a visa or are out with a private car, driver and guide is lunch possible. I have listed two personal recommendations based upon past experience. My choices are:
* Pomorsky is located on Pomorskaya Ulitsa #7 on the third floor and a bit difficult to find on your own. But guides are all familiar with it because it is an outstanding place to dine. They do have an English language menu. The selections are all traditional and I strongly urge you to do a soup, entree and dessert to have the full experience. Their fish soup, borscht and all fish dishes are excellent. There are many meat dishes including chicken, pork, venison and rabbit, but in the far north fish is at its best.
* Restaurant Pochtovaya Kontora is located along the river embankment and is open from Noon to 12 AM, serving both lunch and dinner. The provide a wide array of traditional Russian dishes as well as cuisine that is more in keeping with western European tastes.

If you are out with a driver and guide, you can seek their advice as to what other restaurants are recommended if traditional Russian cuisine is not to your taste.

Arkhangelsk is a memorable experience, but it is a shame that more cruise ships do not make the journey this far east into the high Arctic to enable guests to have the experience.

A map of central Arkhangelsk (© OpenStreetMap contributors)

The skyline of Arkhangelsk seen as the ship docks

The beautiful wood architecture along Chumbarova Avenue

A classic fully restored 18th century wood house

An 18th century wood house that has not been restored, but is still lived in

The historic old St, Nicholas Church

An old church bell tower survives in front of the railway station

19th and 21st century architecture in the Arkhangelsk city center

The story of Nazi bombing of the city in World War II

A modern shopping mall in the Arkhangelsk city center

Statue of Admiral Kuznetzov overlooking the Severnaya Dvina River

Many Arkhangelsk homes rely upon a good stockpile of wood for winter

ABOUT THE AUTHOR

Dr. Lew Deitch

I am a semi-retired professor of geography with over 46 years of teaching experience. During my distinguished career, I directed the Honors Program at Northern Arizona University and developed many programs relating to the study of contemporary world affairs. I am an honors graduate of The University of California, Los Angeles, earned my Master of Arts at The University of Arizona and completed my doctorate in geography at The University of New England in Australia. I am a globetrotter, having visited 92 countries on all continents except Antarctica. My primary focus is upon human landscapes, especially such topics as local architecture, foods, clothing and folk music. I am also a student of world politics and conflict.

I enjoy being in front of an audience, and have spoken to thousands of people at civic and professional organizations. I have been lecturing on board ships for Silversea Cruises since 2008. I love to introduce people to exciting new places both by means of presenting vividly illustrated talks and through serving as a tour consultant for ports of call. I am also an avid writer, and for years I have written my own text books used in my university classes. Now I have turned my attention to writing travel companions, books that will introduce you to the country you are visiting, but not serving as a touring book like the major guides you find in all of the bookstores.

I also love languages, and my skills include a conversational knowledge of German, Russian and Spanish.

I was raised in California, have lived in Canada and Australia. Arizona has been his permanent home since 1974. One exciting aspect of my life was the ten-year period, during which I volunteered my time as an Arizona Highway Patrol reserve trooper, working out on the streets and highways and also developing new safety and enforcement programs for use statewide. I presently live just outside of Phoenix in the beautiful resort city of Scottsdale and still offer a few courses for the local community colleges when I am at home.

I would like to extend an invitation for you to join me on one of the Silversea cruise segments when I am on board presenting my destination talks. You would find it to be a wonderful experience, especially after having read my book on this area, or on the others I have written about.

FOR MORE INFORMATION REGARDING TRAVELING ON BOARD WHEN I AM THE SPEAKER, CONTACT, WESTSIDE INTERNATIONAL TRAVEL, THE TRAVEL AGENCY I USE FOR ALL MY TRAVELS AT:
www.westsideintltravel.com

TO CONTACT ME, PLEASE CHECK OUT MY WEB PAGE FOR MORE INFORMATION AT:
http://www.doctorlew.com

Printed in Poland
by Amazon Fulfillment
Poland Sp. z o.o., Wrocław